SPECTRUM®

Reading

Grade 1

Published by Spectrum®
an imprint of Carson Dellosa Education
Greensboro, NC

Spectrum®
An imprint of Carson Dellosa Education
P.O. Box 35665
Greensboro, NC 27425 USA

ISBN 978-1-4838-1214-4

05-318227784

Table of Contents

Nonfiction: Due to content these pages have more advanced vocabulary. These passages may need to be read with a teacher or parent guide depending on child's reading level.

Little Duck

What is that sound?
What do you think Mama Duck hears?

Something is saying, "Quack, Quack!"
What do you think is making that sound?

That's a funny looking foot!
Whose foot do you think that belongs to?

Hey, it's Little Duck!
How do you think Little Duck feels?

Picture Interpretation and Reading (for all stories): Introduce students to Little Duck, a sweet duckling who is the focus of the following stories. Suggest that the students look at the pictures and talk about what is happening. Have the students relate what they see to their own lives and experiences. Be aware of the vocabulary levels and needs of the group. Key words may be reinforced or developed by writing them on the board as each picture/picture scenario is discussed. First, have students read the story silently by themselves. Help students with any unfamiliar words. Next, have students read the story orally. Discussion questions have been provided to serve as a discussion guide.

Spectrum Reading Grade 1

Beautiful Beginnings

Directions:
Beginning Consonants (1-2): Ask students to say each picture name aloud and listen to the beginning sound. Then, have them write the beginning letter on the line below the picture.
Sequence (3): Have students look at all the pictures. Ask them to write **1** below the event that would happen first, **2** below the event that would happen second, and **3** below the event that would happen third.

Mama Duck

Mama Duck kisses Little Duck on the head. "Hello, Little Duck," she says.

Why does Mama Duck kiss Little Duck?

"Are you hungry, Little Duck?" asks Mama Duck.

Does Little Duck look hungry? How do you know?

Little Duck shakes his head up and down. Little Duck is hungry.

What does it mean when you shake your head up and down?

Mama Duck gives Little Duck some corn to eat.

What do you like to eat?

Beautiful Beginnings

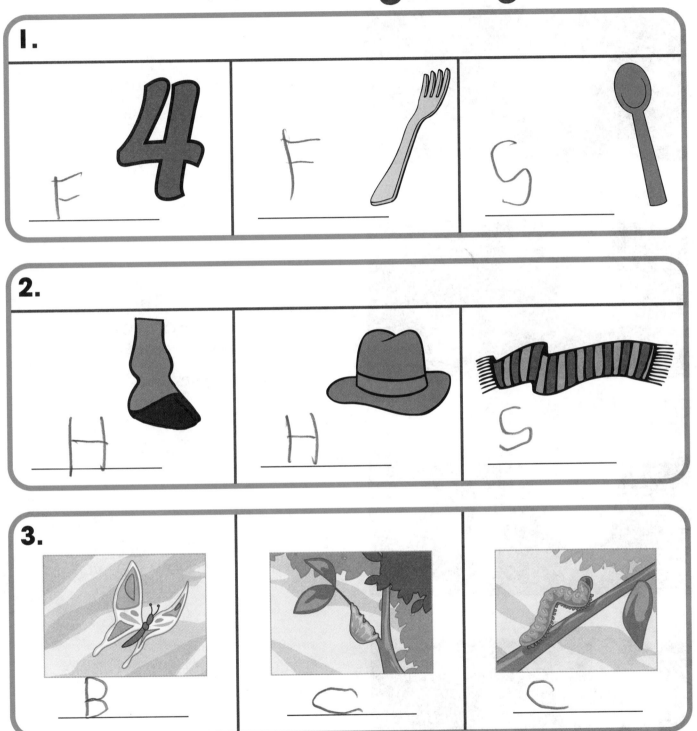

1.

F _____   F _____   S _____

2.

H _____   H _____   S _____

3.

B _____   C _____   C _____

Directions:
Beginning Consonants (1-2): Ask students to say each picture name aloud and listen to the beginning sound. Then, have them write the beginning letter on the line below the picture.
Sequence (3): Have students look at all the pictures. Ask them to write **1** below the event that would happen first, **2** below the event that would happen second, and **3** below the event that would happen third.

Wiggle-Waddle

Little Duck watches his mom walk. Mama Duck walks funny. She moves back and forth in a wiggle.

Why do you think Mama Duck walks that way?

Little Duck laughs. Why does his mom walk that way? Little Duck laughs and laughs.

Why is Little Duck laughing so hard?

"What's so funny, Little Duck?" asks Mama Duck. "Ducks waddle. This is how we walk."

What does it mean to waddle?

Little Duck tries to walk like Mama Duck. He wiggles. He waddles. He wiggle-waddles. Little Duck walks like a duck. Mama Duck is happy.

Why is Mama Duck happy? How do you think Little Duck feels?

Beautiful Beginnings

Directions:

Beginning Consonants (1-2): Ask students to say each picture name aloud and listen to the beginning sound. Then, have them write the beginning letter on the line below the picture.

Sequence (3): Have students look at all the pictures. Ask them to write **1** below the event that would happen first, **2** below the event that would happen second, and **3** below the event that would happen third.

Dinnertime

Little Duck follows his mom to the pond. The pond is very large.

Where is Little Duck going? Why do you think he is going there?

Something moves in the pond. "What was that?" asks Little Duck.

What do you think moved in the pond?

"That's dinner!" says Mama Duck. Then, she quacks loudly.

What do you think will happen next?

A small fish jumps high out of the water and splashes Little Duck.

How do you think Little Duck feels getting splashed?

Beautiful Beginnings

1.

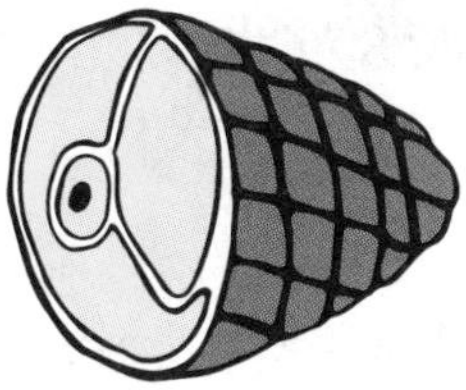

_____   _____   _____

2.

_____   _____   _____

3.

ten	clap
snap	dime
chime	pen
four	score

Directions:
Beginning Consonants (1-2): Ask students to say each picture name aloud and listen to the beginning sound. Then, have them write the beginning letter on the line below the picture.
Rhyme Time (3): Have students draw lines connecting the words that rhyme.

Fish Is Not Dinner

Little Duck shakes the water off his soft feathers. "Who are you?" asks Little Duck.

Why do you think the fish splashes Little Duck?

"I am a fish, Little Duck. I swim in the pond. I am not dinner!"

How do you think the fish feels?

Mama Duck sees something. She waddles ahead. "Come along, Little Duck," she calls.

What do you think Mama Duck sees?

"Well, good-bye, fish," says Little Duck. "I guess we will eat something else for dinner."

Beautiful Beginnings

1.

2.

3.

Directions:

Beginning Consonants (1-2): Ask students to say each picture name aloud and listen to the beginning sound. Then, have them write the beginning letter on the line below the picture.

Sequence (3): Have students look at all the pictures. Ask them to write **1** below the event that would happen first, **2** below the event that would happen second, and **3** below the event that would happen third.

Make Way for Ducklings

Mama Duck walks to the edge of the road. Mama Duck turns her head both ways.

Why does Mama Duck do this?

"Cars make way for ducklings. Follow me, Little Duck," says Mama Duck.

What does Mama Duck mean?

Little Duck turns his head both ways like Mama Duck. Then, he follows Mama Duck across the road.

Why is it important to look both ways?

A boy sees the ducks crossing the road. He shouts, "Hey, make way for ducklings!" Little Duck crosses the road.

Do you think the boy is friendly? Why?

Beautiful Beginnings

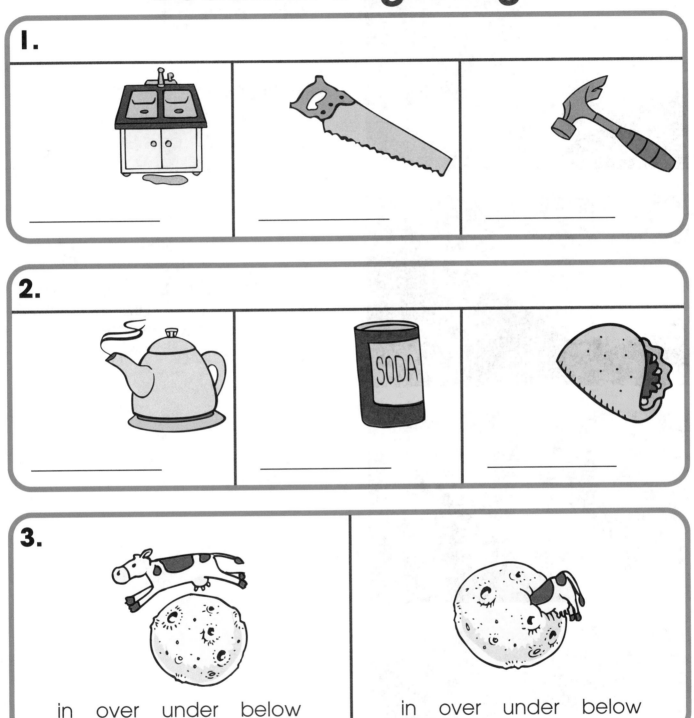

1.

2.

3.

in   over   under   below   in   over   under   below

Directions:
Beginning Consonants (1-2): Ask students to say each picture name aloud and listen to the beginning sound. Then, have them write the beginning letter on the line below the picture.
Using the Pictures (3): Have students look at the pictures. Ask them to circle the word that describes where the cow is located.

A Feast

Little Duck follows Mama Duck up the hill. "Where are we going, Mama Duck?" asks Little Duck.

Where do you think they are going?

"We are going to find some dinner. When the sun sets, it is dinnertime for people and for ducks," says Mama Duck.

What time do you eat dinner?

"Was fish our dinner?" asks Little Duck.

Do you like to eat fish for dinner?

"Not tonight," answers Mama Duck. "Tonight, we have a feast!"

Do you know what a feast is?

Exceptional Endings and Blends

1.

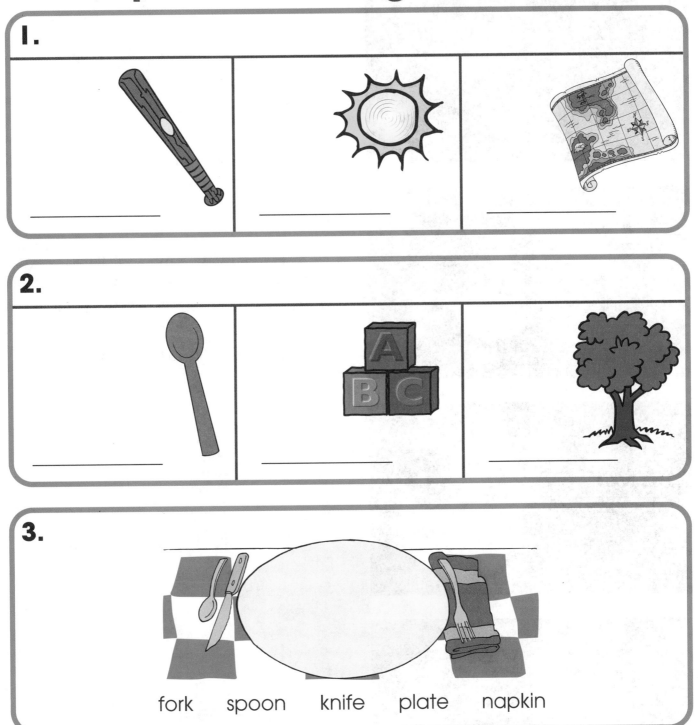

_____   _____   _____

2.

_____   _____   _____

3.

fork   spoon   knife   plate   napkin

Directions:
Ending Consonants (1): Ask students to say each picture name aloud and listen to the ending sound. Then, have them write the ending letter on the line below the picture.
Blends (2): Ask students to say each picture name aloud and listen to the beginning sound. Then, have them write the beginning blend on the line below the picture.
We Go Together (classification) (3): Have students circle the names of the three things that go together.

Bread Crumbs

"What is a feast?" asks Little Duck.

Can feasts be different for different people?

"A feast is a large dinner. Tonight, we are eating something special," says Mama Duck.

What do you think Mama Duck and Little Duck will eat?

"Does it taste like fish?" asks Little Duck.

What would you like to eat at your own feast?

"It tastes better than fish. Tonight, we're having bread crumbs!" she says.

Would you like to eat bread crumbs? Why or why not?

Exceptional Endings and Blends

1.

2.

3.

nest	rock
dock	mother
brother	best
eight	date

Directions:

Ending Consonants (1): Ask students to say each picture name aloud and listen to the ending sound. Then, have them write the ending letter on the line below the picture.

Blends (2): Ask students to say each picture name aloud and listen to the beginning sound. Then, have them write the beginning blend on the line below the picture.

Rhyme Time (3): Have students draw lines connecting the words that rhyme.

Little Duckling?

The boy opens the barn doors. He holds a large pail. The boy smiles at Mama Duck and Little Duck.

What do you think is inside the pail?

"Hello, Mama Duck and Little Duckling," says the boy. The boy reaches into a pail full of bread crumbs.

What do you think the boy will do next?

"Little Duckling?" thought Little Duck. "I am not Little Duckling, I am Little Duck."

Why is Little Duck upset?

The boy holds out his hand. "Come here, Little Duckling. I have some tasty bread crumbs for you."

What should Little Duck do?

Exceptional Endings and Blends

I.

_____   _____   _____

2.

_____   _____   _____

3. It is sharp.
It can hurt you.
Be careful when you use it.
What is it?

An eraser

A pair of scissors

A piece of paper

4. It is chewy.
You can blow bubbles with it.
What is it?

Ice cream

Gum

Soda

Directions:
Ending Consonants (1): Ask students to say each picture name aloud and listen to the ending sound. Then, have them write the ending letter on the line below the picture.
Blends (2): Ask students to say each picture name aloud and listen to the beginning sound. Then, have them write the beginning blend on the line below the picture.
Making Sense (3-4): Ask students to circle the answer that makes the most sense.

Quack, Quack, Quack

Little Duck did not come closer. He was not "Little Duckling." He was Little Duck. And he would not eat bread crumbs if he was not called the right name.

How is Little Duck behaving?

"What's the matter, Little Duckling?" asks the boy. The boy bends down and pats Little Duck's soft head.

Do you think Little Duck likes it when the boy pats his head? Why or why not?

"Wow. You have gotten big," says the boy. "I will call you Little Duck from now on."

Why do you think the boy will call him "Little Duck"?

Little Duck quacks three times. Then, he eats bread crumbs from the boy's hand.

How does Little Duck feel now? How do you know?

Endless Endings

I.

_____   _____   _____

2. school   student   teacher   doctor

3. bird   frog   human   dog

4. circle   two   eight   six

5.

There are four birds.
There are five birds.

6.

There are 5 – 2 toads.
There are 1 + 3 toads.

Directions:
Ending Consonants (1): Ask students to say each picture name aloud and listen to the ending sound. Then, have them write the ending letter on the line below the picture.
Classification (2-4): Have students look at all four pictures or words in each row and then circle the three that belong together.
Using the Pictures (5-6): Have students look at the pictures in each box. Then, have them circle the sentence that describes the picture.

Brrr!

Little Duck dips his foot into the pond. The water is so cold. "Brrr!" says Little Duck.

Have you ever felt cold water like Little Duck?

Mama Duck laughs and says, "It is not cold, Little Duck. Plus, you're a duck. Our feathers keep us warm in cold water."

How do people keep warm when it is cold?

Little Duck wades into the water. The water is cold, but nice. Maybe Little Duck will see the fish again.

Why does Little Duck want to see fish again?

Something strange is in the water. "Mama Duck, what is that?" asks Little Duck.

What do you think is in the water?

More Endings

1.

2.

3. Write a sentence that includes one of the pictures above in #2.

_____

_____

Directions:
Ending Consonants (1): Ask students to say each picture name aloud and listen to the ending sound. Then, have them write the ending letter on the line below the picture.
Blends (2): Ask students to say each picture name aloud and listen to the beginning sound. Then, have them write the beginning blend on the line below the picture.
Writing Time (3): See directions in #3.

New Friend

Little Duck and his mom swim closer to the strange thing. A girl duck pops up from under the water.

Have you ever felt water like Little Duck?

"Wow, that was fun!" says the girl duck. "I love diving in the water."

Do you think she is looking for something? What?

"You don't think it is too cold?" asks Little Duck.

"No," she says. "The water is just right. My name is Matilda. What's yours?"

"My name is Little Duck."

What do you think happens next?

Name_____

Keep on Blending

1.

2.

3.

Directions:

Ending Consonants (1): Ask students to say each picture name aloud and listen to the ending sound. Then, have them write the ending letter on the line below the picture.

Blends (2): Ask students to say each picture name aloud and listen to the beginning sound. Then, have them write the beginning blend on the line below the picture.

Sequence (3): Have students look at all three pictures. Ask them to write **1** below the event that would happen first, **2** below the event that would happen second, and **3** below the event that would happen third.

Snails Away!

"Do you want to dive for snails, Little Duck?" asks Matilda. "They live at the bottom of the pond."

Do you think Little Duck will say yes or no? Why?

"I don't know how to dive," says Little Duck.

"Sure you do. All ducks know how to dive," says Matilda.

Do you think Little Duck will know how to dive? Why?

"I'll try," says Little Duck, and he dives into the water. It is fun underwater. But Little Duck doesn't see any snails.

What other things might Little Duck see underwater?

Little Duck and Matilda come up for air. They didn't catch even one snail. "Well," says Matilda, "there is only one thing to be done."

What do you think Little Duck and Matilda will do next?

Is the End in Sight?

1.

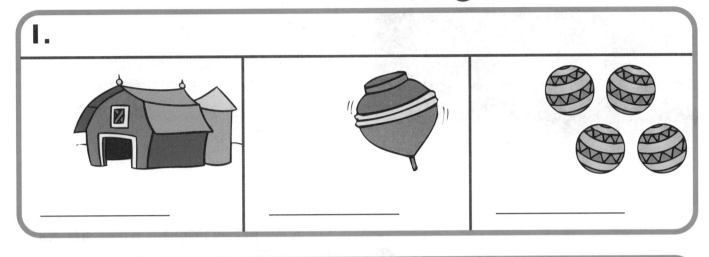

_____ _____ _____

2.

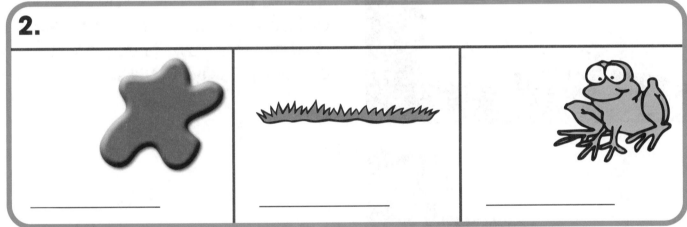

_____ _____ _____

3.

seven	brick
trick	eleven
sneak	leak
treat	beat

Directions:
Ending Consonants (1): Ask students to say each picture name aloud and listen to the ending sound. Then, have them write the ending letter on the line below the picture.
Blends (2): Ask students to say each picture name aloud and listen to the beginning sound. Then, have them write the beginning blend on the line below the picture.
Rhyme Time (3): Have students draw lines connecting the words that rhyme.

Little Duck and Matilda Go to the Farm

Little Duck and Matilda waddle along the side of the road. "Where are we going?" asks Little Duck.

Where do you think they are going?

"We are going to the farm on the hill. The farmer throws away old corn. He throws away stale bread. He throws away grass clippings," says Matilda.

Would you want to eat stale bread? Why or why not?

"What do we do now?" asks Little Duck.

"We will take some of this home with us," says Matilda.

"We are going to make some duck soup," says Matilda.

"Does duck soup taste good?" asks Little Duck.

"Duck soup tastes very good. You'll see," says Matilda.

Do you think duck soup will taste good? Who is telling the story: Matilda, Little Duck, or the author?

Vowels and Digraphs

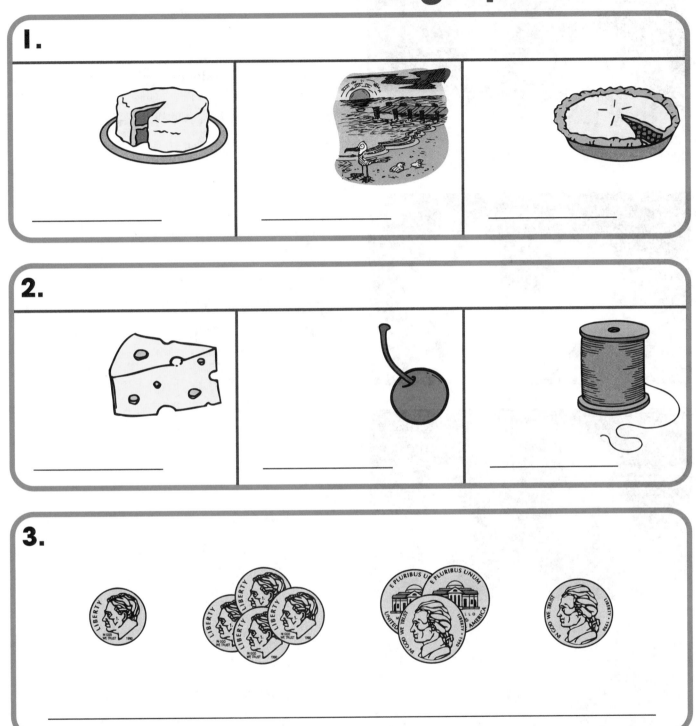

Directions:

Long Vowels (1): Have students name each picture. Then, have them write the long vowel on the line provided.

Dynamite Digraphs (2): Review the **ch** digraph. Have students name each picture. Ask them to write **ch** below each picture that begins with the **ch** sound.

One or More (3): Have students look at all four pictures. Ask them to identify the pictures with only one (singular) object. Tell students to write down their answers.

Duck Soup

Matilda and Little Duck sit by the edge of the pond. "What is in duck soup?" asks Little Duck.

Would you want to eat duck soup? Why or why not?

"Close your eyes and take a guess," says Matilda. "Duck soup is the best soup in the whole world."

What do you think Little Duck tastes?

"I taste corn," says Little Duck, "and I taste bread crumbs. And I taste something green."

What do you think Little Duck tastes that is green?

"Good guess, Little Duck," says Matilda. "Duck soup is made of corn, water, bread crumbs, and grass. Yummy for ducks."

Do you think you would like to eat a bowl of duck soup?

Name_____

Vowels

1.

2.

3.

Directions:
Long Vowels (1): Have students name each picture. Then, have them write the long vowel on the line provided.
Dynamite Digraphs (2): Review the **sh** digraph. Have students name each picture. Ask them to write **sh** below each picture that begins with the **sh** sound.
One or More (3): Have students look at all four pictures. Ask them to identify the pictures with only one (singular) object. Tell students to write down their answers.

Little Duck Dives

Little Duck swims by himself in the pond. Every day, he tries to dive deeper and deeper in the pond.

What do you like to practice?

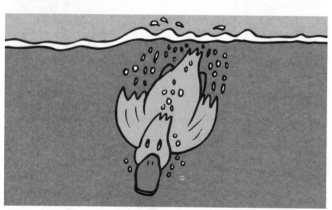

Little Duck wants to find a snail to give to Matilda. One day, he sees something at the bottom of the pond.

What do you think Little Duck sees?

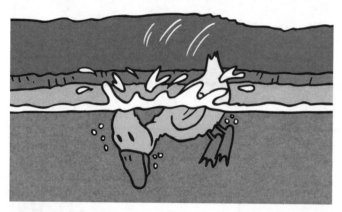

Little Duck swims deeper and deeper to the pond bottom. Something is shiny. It is not a snail.

What do you think is at the bottom?

"What is this?" says Little Duck. He carries a penny in his beak and puts it in the grass.

What do you think Little Duck will do with the penny he found?

Dynamite Digraphs

1.

_____   _____   _____

2.

_____   _____   _____

3.

_____   _____

Directions:
Dynamite Digraphs (1): Review the **th** digraph. Have students name each picture. Ask them to write **th** below each picture that begins with the **th** sound.
Long Vowels (2): Have students name each picture. Then, ask them to write the long vowel on the line provided.
Double Time: Blends and Digraphs (3): Write two words that start with a blend and end with a consonant digraph. Example: French.

What to Do with a Penny

"What should we do with the penny?" asks Little Duck. "Should we add it to the duck soup? Maybe it will taste good with the corn, bread crumbs, and grass?"

What do you think Matilda and Little Duck should do with the penny?

"I don't think you can eat a penny," says Matilda. "Why don't we ask your mom if she knows what to do with it?"

What do you think Mama Duck will say?

Little Duck and Matilda waddle over to Mama Duck. "Mama Duck, what should we do with a penny?" asks Little Duck.

What are some things you would do with a penny?

"Well, you should throw the penny back into the pond and make a wish," says Mama Duck.

Would you want to throw the penny back and make a wish?

Dynamite Digraphs

1.

_____   _____   _____

2.

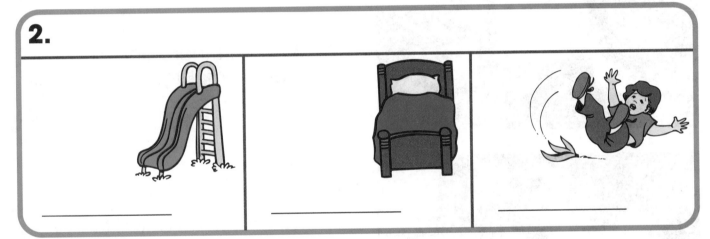

_____   _____   _____

3.

_____ The crowd cheers.

_____ The batter comes to the plate.

_____ The batter strikes out.

Directions:
Dynamite Digraphs (1): Review the **wh** digraph. Have students name each picture. Ask them to write **wh** below each picture that begins with the **wh** sound.
Vowels (2): Have students name each picture. Then, ask students to write the vowel on the line provided.
Sequence (3): Have students read all three sentences. Ask them to write **1** next to the event that would happen first, **2** next to the event that would happen second, and **3** next to the event that would happen third.

Make a Wish, Little Duck

"What should I wish for?" asks Little Duck. "I already have everything I want. I have the best Mama Duck, and I have a best friend."

What would you wish for?

"Well, isn't there anything else you want, Little Duck?" asks Mama Duck.

What could Little Duck wish for?

"I guess I wish I could fly like the big ducks in the sky," says Little Duck. He throws the penny back in the pond.

Do you think Little Duck makes a good wish? How come?

"But Little Duck, your wish has already come true. You can fly!" says Mama Duck and kisses him on the head.

What other animals can fly?

Beautiful Beginnings

1.

2.

3.

4.

5.

6.

7.

Directions:
Vowels (1): Have students name each picture. Then, have them write the vowel on the line provided.
Dynamite Digraphs (2-7): Have students name each picture. Ask them to write the digraph or blend used in each word below each picture.

Little Duck Is Scared

Little Duck stands at the edge of the pond. "I am scared, Mama Duck. What if I fall? I don't think I can fly," says Little Duck.

Will it be bad if Little Duck falls? Why or why not?

"Little Duck, don't think so much," says Mama Duck. "Just count one, two, three. Then, spread your wings and flap them up and down. Soon, you will be flying."

Do you think Little Duck can fly? How come?

Little Duck counts, "One, two, three." He flaps his wings and stops. "I just can't do this. I am not like the other ducks."

Do you think Little Duck is right? How come?

"Come on, Little Duck," says Matilda. "We can try together." Matilda flaps her wings. "One, two, three!" Matilda is flying. Little Duck watches from the ground.

Go Short or Go Long: Aa

1. ate _____

2. at _____

3. ape _____

4. act _____

5. ant _____

6. age _____

7. rake _____

8. ray _____

9. able _____

10. rat _____

11. rack _____

12. rate _____

13. Andy _____

14. Alex _____

15. Abe _____

Directions:
Vowels (1-15): Have students say each word aloud. Then, have them write **short** or **long** next to the word to tell if it contains a short or a long a sound.

Little Duck Tries

Little Duck looks up at Matilda. She is flying in the sky. "Come on, Little Duck. I know you can do it!" she calls.

Do you think Little Duck can fly? How do you know?

"Just try, Little Duck," says Mama Duck. "Count one, two, three, and flap your wings. I know you can do it, too."

Are you ever afraid to try something new? How do you think Little Duck is feeling? Why?

Little Duck looks at his mom. Next, he looks at Matilda flying in the sky. "Okay. I will try," says Little Duck.

How are Mama Duck and Matilda helping Little Duck?

Little Duck starts to flap his wings. "One," he says, and lifts his wings. "Two," he says, and lifts them again. "Threeeeeeee!" Little Duck flies!

How do you think Little Duck feels about himself? How do you know?

Go Short or Go Long: Ee

1. pen _____

2. pencil _____

3. plea _____

4. pea _____

5. glee _____

6. green _____

7. tea _____

8. ten _____

9. teen _____

10. hen _____

11. fence _____

12. bee _____

13. be _____

14. bend _____

15. Ben _____

Directions:
Vowels (1-15): Have students say each word aloud. Then, ask them to write **short** or **long** next to the word to tell if it contains a short or a long e sound.

Little Duck and Matilda Fly

Little Duck and Matilda are flying. "Wow! This is fun!" says Little Duck.

"I knew you would like it," says Matilda.

Do you think flying would be fun? Why or why not?

Little Duck flaps his wings harder. He moves higher in the sky. Next, he glides through the air. Little Duck moves his wings slower. Now, he moves closer to the ground.

Have you ever watched ducks fly? What was it like?

"Wow! I think I get it! I think I know how to fly," says Little Duck.

"You are doing great!" says Matilda. "Just watch out for clouds."

"Why?" asks Little Duck.

Why should Little Duck watch out for clouds?

Little Duck turns to look at Matilda. He does not see the cloud ahead. "Little Duck! Watch out!" calls Matilda. Little Duck flies right into a giant cloud.

What do you think will happen next?

Go Short or Go Long: Ii

1. pie _____

2. pin _____

3. pine _____

4. pink _____

5. pit _____

6. tin _____

7. time _____

8. tiny _____

9. tick _____

10. Tim _____

11. die _____

12. dim _____

13. diet _____

14. dine _____

15. dinner _____

Directions:
Vowels (1-15): Have students say each word aloud. Then, ask them to write **short** or **long** next to the word to tell if it contains a short or a long i sound.

A Cloud

Little Duck flies into a cloud. He can't see anything. Everything is white and hazy. The air gets bumpy, too. "Oh, no!" calls Little Duck.

What is happening?

Little Duck starts to fall. He tumbles around and around. Little Duck is falling out of the cloud. He is falling through the sky. He is falling toward the hard ground.

What should Little Duck do?

"Little Duck, flap your wings! Flap your wings hard," calls Matilda. Little Duck is so dizzy. He keeps falling and falling. Little Duck is close to the ground.

Why is Little Duck so dizzy?

"Little Duck, you must flap your wings!" calls Mama Duck. Little Duck sucks in air. He flaps one wing. He flaps the other. "Flap harder, Little Duck! Flap harder!" Little Duck flaps his wings as fast as he can.

What will happen to Little Duck?

Go Short or Go Long: Oo

1. pot _____

2. spot _____

3. snow _____

4. not _____

5. oat _____

6. on _____

7. box _____

8. mop _____

9. rope _____

10. Oliver _____

11. show _____

12. shop _____

13. hot _____

14. stop _____

15. slope _____

Directions:
Vowels (1-15): Have students say each word aloud. Then, ask them to write **short** or **long** next to the word to tell if it contains a short or a long o sound.

Little Duck Soars

Little Duck flaps his wings as hard as he can. He shoots up in the air again! "Good job, Little Duck! Good job!" calls Mama Duck from the ground.

How do you think Mama Duck feels? How do you know?

Little Duck flaps his wings. Little Duck shakes his head. He calls to Mama Duck below, "It's okay, Mama Duck! It's okay!"

Matilda flies next to him. "Oh my, Little Duck! You scared me. Are you all right?" she asks.

Little Duck smiles. "Yup. I'll try never to fly into a cloud again. But I can really fly, Matilda! I can do it!"

How is Little Duck feeling?

Little Duck is so happy. He flaps his wings hard. He shoots higher and higher in the sky. "Yea!" he shouts. "Honk, honk!" he calls. Matilda and Mama Duck watch him soar.

What has changed about Little Duck?

Name_____

Go Short or Go Long: Uu

1. under _____

2. cube _____

3. umbrella _____

4. cut _____

5. cute _____

6. butter _____

7. yummy _____

8. mule _____

9. club _____

10. duck _____

11. dune _____

12. tuck _____

13. tune _____

14. run _____

15. funny _____

Directions:
Vowels (1-15): Have students say each word aloud. Then, ask them to write **short** or **long** next to the word to tell if it contains a short or a long u sound.

Spectrum Reading Grade 1

Big Time Rhyme

1. funny

2. honey

3. duck

4. stop

5. ton

6. snow

7. bear

8. spring

9. fall

10. tell

11. tear

Directions:
Rhyme Time (1-11): Have students draw lines connecting the words to the pictures that rhyme.

Classified Information

1. sad   glad   mad   cage

2. five   alive   nine   thirteen

3. boat   don't   won't   did

4. wheat   seat   beat   cat

5. pie   pine   pin   spine

6. jump   true   cube   June

7. oat   coat   spot   moat

8. glee   green   gem   greet

9. hen   ten   tent   teen

10. ray   rat   rake   rate

Directions:
Grouping Together (1-10): Have students read all four words in each line. Then, tell them to circle the three words that share the same vowel sound.

Carolyn Dreams of a Pet

Carolyn looked around her room. There were animals everywhere. She had teddy bears from her grandma. She had stuffed animals from her aunt. She even had posters of puppies on the wall. But what Carolyn wanted was a real pet. She wanted a kitten or a puppy to love and play with.

What do you dream of? Do you have a pet? Would you want one?

Reading Skills

1. This story is about

   _____ Carolyn wanting a pet.

   _____ Carolyn wanting a toy.

   _____ how Carolyn is sad.

2. Carolyn has posters on the walls of

   _____ horses.   _____ puppies.   _____ flowers.

3. The **setting** is where a story takes place. What is the setting for this story?

   _____ Carolyn's kitchen

   _____ Carolyn's living room

   _____ Carolyn's bedroom

4. In the picture on page 50, how does Carolyn look?

   _____ sad   _____ happy   _____ bored

Thinking Further and Predicting Outcomes

1. Do you think Carolyn will get a real pet or more teddy bears? How come?

Directions:
Reading Skills Finding the main idea **(1):** Have students read the question and mark the correct answer. Story Details or Cause and Effect **(2-4):** Have students read the question and mark the correct answer.
Thinking Further and Predicting Outcomes (1): Have students read each question, and then on a separate piece of paper write down and/or discuss their thoughts, opinions, and predictions. As the stories progress, have students discuss whether their predictions were accurate.

Carolyn Talks to Her Mom

Carolyn's mom was reading a book in the den. "Mom, can I ask you something?" asked Carolyn.

"Sure, honey," said Mrs. Jones.

"Mom, I know I have teddy bears from Grandma. I even have stuffed animals from Aunt Linda. But I really want a pet I can hold and take care of," said Carolyn.

Carolyn's mom put down her book. "Pets take a lot of work," said Mrs. Jones. "And you don't just take care of a pet for a day, or a week, or even a month. Pets are part of the family for years. Do you think you would have time to take care of a pet? Why don't you really think about it."

Do you have a pet? Do you think pets are hard to take care of?

Reading Skills

1. This story is about

_____ Carolyn hearing about how pets are bad.

_____ Carolyn hearing about how pets take work.

_____ Carolyn hearing about how dirty pets are.

2. Carolyn's aunt's name is _____ Lucinda. _____ Lucy. _____ Linda.

3. What does Mrs. Jones want Carolyn to do?

_____ get a new stuffed animal

_____ think about whether she is ready for a pet

_____ forget about getting a pet

4. Carolyn comes to talk to Mom while Mom is

_____ reading.   _____ working.   _____ napping.

Thinking Further and Predicting Outcomes

1. Do you think Carolyn would take good care of a pet? How come?

2. Do you think Carolyn's mother will help her get a pet? How come?

Directions:
Reading Skills Finding the main idea **(1):** Have students read the question and mark the correct answer. Story Details or Cause and Effect **(2-4):** Have students read the question and mark the correct answer.
Thinking Further and Predicting Outcomes (1-2): Have students read each question, and then on a separate piece of paper write down and/or discuss their thoughts, opinions, and predictions. As the stories progress, have students discuss whether their predictions were accurate.

Time for a Pet

Carolyn went back to her room. She had just started school. Her new teacher gave her lots of homework. She had books to read and stories to write. Her class was even going to put on a school play.

Maybe she didn't have time to take care of a pet after all. Carolyn held her teddy bear tight. "What do you think I should do, teddy bear?" she asked. But the teddy bear didn't say anything at all because he wasn't real.

Do you think Carolyn has time to take care of a pet? Why or why not?

Reading Skills

1. In this story,

_____ Carolyn thinks that she will have lots of time to care for a pet.

_____ Carolyn thinks she might not have enough time for a pet.

_____ Carolyn decides she doesn't want a pet.

2. Carolyn talks to her

_____ aunt.   _____ teddy bear.   _____ posters.

3. In this story, Carolyn feels

_____ excited.   _____ worried.   _____ mad.

4. Which of these is NOT something that takes up Carolyn's time?

_____ soccer practice _____ homework _____ a school play

Thinking Further and Predicting Outcomes

1. Do you think Carolyn can handle both a pet and school work?

2. Do you think if Carolyn gets a pet, she will take good care of it?

3. If Carolyn had a pet, do you think she would talk to it? Why or why not?

Directions:
Reading Skills Finding the main idea **(1):** Have students read the question and mark the correct answer. Story Details or Cause and Effect **(2-4):** Have students read the question and mark the correct answer.
Thinking Further and Predicting Outcomes (1-3): Have students read each question, and then on a separate piece of paper write down and/or discuss their thoughts, opinions, and predictions. As the stories progress, have students discuss whether their predictions were accurate.

Knock, Knock

"Knock, knock," said Carolyn's dad. He stood in the doorway. "Hi, Carolyn. Mom said you wanted a pet. What kind of pet did you want?"

"Hi, Dad. I want a pet that is soft, like a kitten or a puppy," said Carolyn.

"Well, pets like dogs and cats are a lot of work," said Mr. Jones. "How about a pet turtle or a fish tank with lots of pretty fish? We could get a blue fish or maybe even an orange and white clown fish. What do you say?"

But Carolyn was sad. She knew she could never hug a turtle or a fish.

What is your favorite animal? Do some animals make better pets than others?

Reading Skills

1. In this story,

_____ Carolyn's dad tells her she can't have a pet.

_____ Carolyn's dad talks about other types of pets.

_____ Carolyn's dad says he will get her a dog.

2. Carolyn's dad mentions a possible pet. It is a

_____ turtle.   _____ bunny.   _____ pony.

3. Who is the main character in the story?

_____ Mrs. Jones

_____ Mr. Jones

_____ Carolyn

4. Carolyn's mom and dad _____ about pets being a lot of work.

_____ agree   _____ do not agree

Thinking Further and Predicting Outcomes

1. Do you think Carolyn would enjoy a pet turtle?

2. Do you think Carolyn's dad knows why she wants a pet? Why or why not?

Directions:
Reading Skills Finding the main idea (**1**): Have students read the question and mark the correct answer. Story Details or Cause and Effect (**2-4**): Have students read the question and mark the correct answer.
Thinking Further and Predicting Outcomes (1-2): Have students read each question, and then on a separate piece of paper write down and/or discuss their thoughts, opinions, and predictions. As the stories progress, have students discuss whether their predictions were accurate.

I Promise

Carolyn sat down for breakfast with her mom and dad. She filled her bowl with cereal. "Mom and Dad," said Carolyn, "I know I can take care of a pet. I will help feed it every morning. I will fill its bowl with water. I promise, I will always take care of it. We can name our pet 'Promise.'"

Carolyn's mom and dad looked at each other. Carolyn's mom said, "Wow, you make a good case for a pet. Dad and I will have a long talk. We will tell you our answer tomorrow."

What do you think Carolyn's parents will say? Explain your answer.

Reading Skills

1. In this story,

_____ Carolyn explains how she would take care of her new pet.

_____ Carolyn says she is sad.

_____ Carolyn talks about her friends at school.

2. The pet will be named _____ Prince. _____ Promise. _____ Misty.

3. This story takes place

_____ in the morning. _____ at lunchtime. _____ before bed.

4. When will Carolyn's parents tell her their answer?

_____ tomorrow _____ Monday _____ after lunch

5. Who is telling the story?

_____ Carolyn _____ the author _____ Carolyn's mom

Thinking Further and Predicting Outcomes

1. Do you think Carolyn has explained herself well? How do you know?

2. Do you think Carolyn's parents like her plan? Why or why not?

Directions:
Reading Skills Finding the main idea **(1):** Have students read the question and mark the correct answer. Story Details or Cause and Effect **(2-5):** Have students read the question and mark the correct answer.
Thinking Further and Predicting Outcomes (1-2): Have students read each question, and then on a separate piece of paper write down and/or discuss their thoughts, opinions, and predictions. As the stories progress, have students discuss whether their predictions were accurate.

Yes or No?

All night, Carolyn tossed in her bed. She knew she could take care of a pet. She hoped her parents would say yes. She would give her pet fresh water. She would brush its fur. And she would always love it.

Carolyn's last name was Jones. So her new pet would be named "Promise Jones." She liked the name already.

Carolyn ran down the stairs at 7:00 in the morning. "Wow, you are up early!" said Carolyn's mom.

"Can we get Promise?" asked Carolyn.

"Let's call your dad in the kitchen and see," said Carolyn's mom.

Why do you think Carolyn tossed in her bed all night? Why did she get up so early?

Reading Skills

I. This story is about

_____ Carolyn waking up early to find out if she will get a pet.

_____ Carolyn waking up early to go to school.

_____ Carolyn sleeping because she is so tired.

2. Carolyn's last name is _____ Jones. _____ Promise. _____ Linda.

3. Which of these is NOT something Carolyn will do for her pet?

_____ brush its fur

_____ love it

_____ clip its nails

4. Look at the picture on page 60. Carolyn looks

_____ excited.   _____ sneaky.   _____ grumpy.

Thinking Further and Predicting Outcomes

I. What will the decision be?

2. Why do people love pets?

3. How do you think Carolyn feels as she comes running down the stairs?

Directions:
Reading Skills Finding the main idea **(I):** Have students read the question and mark the correct answer. Story Details or Cause and Effect **(2-4):** Have students read the question and mark the correct answer.
Thinking Further and Predicting Outcomes (I-3): Have students read each question, and then on a separate piece of paper write down and/or discuss their thoughts, opinions, and predictions. As the stories progress, have students discuss whether their predictions were accurate.

A Real Pet

Carolyn's dad walked into the kitchen. He had a big smile on his face. Carolyn was jumping in her seat. Her dad smiled like that when he said something good.

"Carolyn, your mom and I have talked all night about a pet," said her dad. "Now, if you promise to take good care of a pet, we will get one."

Carolyn ran to her dad and hugged him. Carolyn's mom joined the hug. The Jones family would soon have a real pet.

Why do you think Carolyn's parents said yes? Do you think Carolyn will keep her promise?

Reading Skills

1. This story is about

_____ Carolyn finding out that she will get a pet.

_____ Carolyn finding out that she will not get a pet.

_____ Carolyn finding out she's late for school.

2. Carolyn hugged her _____ mother. _____ father. _____ parents.

3. Carolyn's dad has a big smile on his face when he has something _____ to say.

_____ strange   _____ good   _____ bad

4. What is the setting for this story?

_____ the kitchen

_____ the den

_____ Carolyn's bedroom

Thinking Further and Predicting Outcomes

1. Where will the Jones family get their pet?

2. Do you think Carolyn's parents made the right decision? How come?

Directions:
Reading Skills Finding the main idea **(1):** Have students read the question and mark the correct answer. Story Details or Cause and Effect **(2-4):** Have students read the question and mark the correct answer.
Thinking Further and Predicting Outcomes (1-2): Have students read each question, and then on a separate piece of paper write down and/or discuss their thoughts, opinions, and predictions. As the stories progress, have students discuss whether their predictions were accurate.

Today a Pet

"Carolyn, after school we will go to the pound. There, we will look for a pet that needs a home," said Mrs. Jones.

Carolyn was so excited in school. "I'm going to get a pet today!" Carolyn told her friends.

"What kind of pet are you going to get?" asked her friend Freddy. "Will you get an alligator?"

"Nope," said Carolyn.

"Will you get a goldfish?" asked Freddy.

"Nope," said Carolyn.

"I hope to get a kitten or a puppy," said Carolyn.

Would an alligator make a good pet? Would a goldfish make a good pet? Why or why not?

Reading Skills

1. This story is about

_____ Carolyn telling her friends about getting a pet.

_____ Carolyn telling her friends about her school project.

_____ Carolyn's visit to the pound.

2. What was the name of Carolyn's friend who asked about her new pet? His name is

_____ Freddy.   _____ Eddie.   _____ Betty.

3. Carolyn tells Freddy that she would like to get a puppy or

_____ an alligator.

_____ a kitten.

_____ a goldfish.

4. Where will the Jones family go to get a pet?

_____ the pound   _____ the pet store   _____ a farm

Thinking Further and Predicting Outcomes

1. Do you think Carolyn will show her pet to her classmates? Why or why not?

Directions:
Reading Skills Finding the main idea (**1**): Have students read the question and mark the correct answer. Story Details or Cause and Effect (**2-4**): Have students read the question and mark the correct answer.
Thinking Further and Predicting Outcomes (1): Have students read each question, and then on a separate piece of paper write down and/or discuss their thoughts, opinions, and predictions. As the stories progress, have students discuss whether their predictions were accurate.

Two Good Things

"Mom, why are we going to the pound? Shouldn't we go to the pet store?" said Carolyn.

"The pound is an animal shelter. It is a place where lost or unwanted animals are brought," said Mrs. Jones. "These animals really need homes. If we can find an animal here, two good things happen. We get a family pet, and an animal gets a home. The pound has all types of animals. We will see cats, dogs, and even some rabbits."

What would you do if you found a lost animal? Who would you tell?

Reading Skills

1. This story is about

_____ Carolyn learning about the pound.

_____ Carolyn wanting to go to the pet store.

_____ Carolyn changing her mind about getting a pet.

2. Mrs. Jones and Carolyn will go to the

_____ pound.   _____ pet store.   _____ zoo.

3. In the picture above, what is Carolyn thinking about?

_____ a stuffed dog   _____ a teddy bear   _____ a real dog

4. Which kind of animal will Carolyn and her mom NOT see at the pound?

_____ cats   _____ rabbits   _____ chickens

Thinking Further and Predicting Outcomes

1. Do you think it's a good idea to go to the pound for a pet? Why or why not?

2. What will Carolyn do when she chooses her pet?

Directions:
Reading Skills Finding the main idea **(1):** Have students read the question and mark the correct answer. Story Details or Cause and Effect **(2-4):** Have students read the question and mark the correct answer.
Thinking Further and Predicting Outcomes (1-2): Have students read each question, and then on a separate piece of paper write down and/or discuss their thoughts, opinions, and predictions. As the stories progress, have students discuss whether their predictions were accurate.

The Pound

Carolyn and her mom walked into a large room filled with rows of cages. Behind the bars were animals of all shapes and sizes. There were fat dogs, skinny dogs like hot dogs, furry dogs, and cages of cats. Carolyn reached her hand through the bars.

She petted a sleeping kitten. Its tummy was moving up and down. Next, a fat cat licked Carolyn's hand. Its tongue felt scratchy on her hand.

What animal do you think Carolyn will pick? Why?

Name_____

1. This story is about

_____ Carolyn seeing all sorts of animals at the pound.

_____ Carolyn feeling scared.

_____ Carolyn playing with a lizard.

2. Carolyn pets a kitten that is

_____ eating.   _____ sleeping.   _____ drinking.

3. How did the fat cat's tongue feel on Carolyn's hand?

_____ scratchy   _____ soft   _____ slimy

4. There was only one kind of animal at the pound.

_____ true

_____ false

Thinking Further and Predicting Outcomes

1. Will Carolyn choose a pet after all? How do you know?

2. Will Carolyn get more than one pet? How do you know?

3. What kinds of words are used to describe the dogs?

Directions:
Reading Skills Finding the main idea **(1):** Have students read the question and mark the correct answer. Story Details or Cause and Effect **(2-4):** Have students read the question and mark the correct answer.
Thinking Further and Predicting Outcomes (1-3): Have students read each question, and then on a separate piece of paper write down and/or discuss their thoughts, opinions, and predictions. As the stories progress, have students discuss whether their predictions were accurate.

Carolyn Is Sad

"Mom, who feeds all these animals?"

"The workers here feed them, but there are not enough people to brush them, or even love them."

"Mom, this makes me sad," said Carolyn.

"I know Carolyn, but we can only take one pet. And saving one animal is a good thing," said Mrs. Jones.

"Yes," said Carolyn, and she kept looking at all the cages.

Why does Carolyn feel sad? What does Mrs. Jones say that makes Carolyn feel better?

Reading Skills

1. This story is about

_____ Carolyn realizing that taking care of only one pet is still a good thing.

_____ Carolyn realizing that she should take five pets.

_____ Carolyn leaving the pound with no pets.

2. The pets are living in ____ cages. ____ houses. ____ boxes.

3. The pound needs more

_____ cats. _____ dogs. _____ workers.

4. Carolyn wishes that all the animals had someone to _____ them.

_____ wash _____ love _____ name

Thinking Further and Predicting Outcomes

1. Do you think Carolyn will feel better about taking only one pet? How come?

2. Do you think Carolyn is a caring person? Why or why not?

3. The next time Carolyn gets a pet, do you think she will go to the pound again? Why or why not?

Directions:
Reading Skills Finding the main idea **(1):** Have students read the question and mark the correct answer. Story Details or Cause and Effect **(2-4):** Have students read the question and mark the correct answer.
Thinking Further and Predicting Outcomes (1-3): Have students read each question, and then on a separate piece of paper write down and/or discuss their thoughts, opinions, and predictions. As the stories progress, have students discuss whether their predictions were accurate.

Promise Jones

Carolyn did not know what to do. So many animals needed a home, and she could take only one. Carolyn went back to the sleeping kitten. It looked like a baby cloud. It was a tiny ball of soft fur. She reached her hand in the cage and petted it slowly. "I think I will take you," she said. "Your name will be Promise Jones." Just then, the kitten looked up at Carolyn.

Why do you think Carolyn chooses the kitten? What animal would you have picked? Do you think Carolyn picked a good name for her new pet? Why or why not?

Reading Skills

I. This story is about

_____ Carolyn choosing a kitten.

_____ Carolyn choosing a puppy.

_____ Carolyn choosing two puppies.

2. What color is the kitten? _____ white _____ black _____ brown

3. Which sentence is true?

_____ Mom had to choose for Carolyn.

_____ Carolyn chose the sleeping kitten.

_____ Carolyn decided to get a kitten and a puppy.

4. Carolyn thinks the kitten looks like

_____ a baby cloud. _____ a snowball. _____ a cotton ball.

Thinking Further and Predicting Outcomes

I. Do you think Carolyn will always take good care of her kitten? How come?

2. Do you think Carolyn will be happy with her new pet? Why or why not?

Directions:
Reading Skills Finding the main idea **(1):** Have students read the question and mark the correct answer. Story Details or Cause and Effect **(2-4):** Have students read the question and mark the correct answer.
Thinking Further and Predicting Outcomes (1-2): Have students read each question, and then on a separate piece of paper write down and/or discuss their thoughts, opinions, and predictions. As the stories progress, have students discuss whether their predictions were accurate.

A New Kitten

"Mom, I think this is our new pet," said Carolyn.

Carolyn's mom bent down and looked into the kitten's cage.

"Yes, he is a beautiful little kitten. I think he will like being part of our family. Let's tell the man at the desk that we have found our new pet," said Mrs. Jones.

The man behind the desk said, "New kittens need shots before they can go home with you. You can pick up your boy kitten tomorrow. He will need cat food, water, and a soft place to sleep."

Why do pets need shots? What else might a new kitten like to have?

Name_____

Reading Skills

1. In this story,

_____ Carolyn realizes she cannot have her kitten until tomorrow.

_____ Carolyn learns that the kitten belongs to someone.

_____ Carolyn learns that the kitten is 3 years old.

2. The kitten is a _____ boy. _____ girl.

3. Before the kitten can come home with Carolyn, it needs to have its _____.

_____ food   _____ shots   _____ training

4. Mrs. Jones thinks that the kitten is

_____ too little.   _____ too wild.   _____ beautiful.

Thinking Further and Predicting Outcomes

1. Do you think Carolyn will be upset that she can't have the kitten right away? How come?

2. Do you think Carolyn will be nervous for the kitten because he needs shots? How come?

Directions:
Reading Skills Finding the main idea **(1):** Have students read the question and mark the correct answer. Story Details or Cause and Effect **(2-4):** Have students read the question and mark the correct answer.
Thinking Further and Predicting Outcomes (1-2): Have students read each question, and then on a separate piece of paper write down and/or discuss their thoughts, opinions, and predictions. As the stories progress, have students discuss whether their predictions were accurate.

A Gift

Carolyn's dad was waiting at the front door of the house. He had a gift in his hand. Carolyn ran to her dad. "Dad, our new kitten comes tomorrow! He is so soft! He looks just like a cotton ball or a cloud," said Carolyn.

"Should we still call him Promise? If he is so soft, maybe we should call him Cloudy or Mr. Cotton," said Carolyn's dad.

"No. I already told him his name was Promise Jones," said Carolyn.

"Well, I bought food, litter, a litter box, and a gift for Promise Jones," said Carolyn's dad.

Carolyn unwrapped the gift. It was a soft cat bed shaped in a circle. A kitten would feel safe and warm inside it. Carolyn hugged her dad. "Promise Jones will love his new bed," she said.

What is the most important thing a new pet would need?

Name_____

Reading Skills

1. This story is about

_____ Carolyn getting a gift from her dad.

_____ Carolyn learning to study.

_____ Carolyn playing with Promise.

2. The new kitten is like a

_____ cotton ball.   _____ paper.   _____ snow.

3. Carolyn's dad asks if they should call the kitten Cloudy or

_____ Buttons.   _____ Snowy.   _____ Mr. Cotton.

4. What does Mr. Jones buy as a gift for Promise Jones?

_____ a cat bed   _____ a scratching post   _____ litter

Thinking Further and Predicting Outcomes

1. Do you think Carolyn makes the right decision about keeping Promise's name the same? Why?

2. Do you like soft things? Why?

3. If you got a kitten, what would you name it?

Directions:
Reading Skills Finding the main idea (1): Have students read the question and mark the correct answer. Story Details or Cause and Effect (2-4): Have students read the question and mark the correct answer.
Thinking Further and Predicting Outcomes (1-3): Have students read each question, and then on a separate piece of paper write down and/or discuss their thoughts, opinions, and predictions. As the stories progress, have students discuss whether their predictions were accurate.

Promise Jones Comes Home

The next day, Promise Jones came home. Carolyn and her mom and dad sat in the family room. Slowly, they opened the kitten carrier.

First, one tiny, white foot pressed on the rug. Then, another tiny foot came out. Next came Promise Jones' head poking out of the carrier. "Hi, Promise Jones," said Carolyn. She held out her hand. Promise looked around the room.

"Meow," he said. He walked over to Carolyn. Carolyn held him in her arms. Then, she kissed his tiny head. Carolyn said, "Promise Jones, you have found a home. We promise."

Do you think Carolyn and her family will be happy with their new pet? Why or why not? Do you think Carolyn will keep her promise with her new kitten?

Name_____

Reading Skills

1. This story is about

_____ Carolyn promising to care for her cat.

_____ Carolyn eating dinner with her cat.

_____ Carolyn having a party with her parents.

2. Carolyn plays with her new pet in the

_____ bedroom.   _____ family room.   _____ kitchen.

3. How do you think Promise Jones felt?

_____ shy   _____ sad   _____ lazy

4. What is Carolyn's promise to her new kitten?

_____ She will play with him every day.

_____ She will not get any more pets.

_____ He has found a home.

Thinking Further and Predicting Outcomes

1. Do you think Carolyn will ever want another pet? Why?

2. Would you want somebody like Carolyn as your friend? Why or why not?

Directions:
Reading Skills Finding the main idea **(1):** Have students read the question and mark the correct answer. Story Details or Cause and Effect **(2-4):** Have students read the question and mark the correct answer.
Thinking Further and Predicting Outcomes (1-2): Have students read each question, and then on a separate piece of paper write down and/or discuss their thoughts, opinions, and predictions. As the stories progress, have students discuss whether their predictions were accurate.

Name_____

Revisiting

1.

_____ _____ _____

2.

_____ _____ _____

3. It has lots of animals.
It is fun to visit.
You can learn a lot.
What is it?

a school

a zoo

the moon

4. You can swim here.
It feels cool. Have fun!
What is it?

a pool

a bathtub

a glass of water

Directions:

Blends (1-2): Ask students to say each picture aloud and listen to the beginning sound. Have them write the beginning blend on the line below the picture.

Making Sense (3-4): Ask students to circle the answer that makes the most sense.

Spectrum Reading Grade 1

Finding the Correct Word

1. Do you like to _____ songs?

sing

sings

sang

2. The duck enjoys _____ corn.

eaten

eating

to eat

3. Jimmy has _____ into the pool.

jumping

jumped

jump

4. Josefina _____ to play piano.

like

likes

liking

5.

_____

_____

_____

_____

_____

_____

Directions:

Sentence Completion (1-4): Have students circle the word that best completes the sentence.

Sequence (5): Have the student look at all six pictures. Ask the student to write **1** below the event that would happen first, **2** below the event that would happen second, and so on.

Blends Review

1.
_____ _____

2.
_____ _____

3.
_____ _____

4.
_____ _____

5.
_____ _____

6.
_____ _____

7.
_____ _____

8.
_____ _____

Directions:

Blends and Ending Consonants (1-8): Have the student look at each picture and say it aloud. Ask them to listen to the beginning blends and ending consonants. Then, have him or her write down the beginning blends and ending consonants next to each word.

Blends Review

1.

_____   _____   _____

2.

_____   _____   _____

3.

zba ____ ____ ____   hia ____ ____ ____

guk ____ ____ ____   bnu ____ ____ ____

Directions:
Beginning Consonants (1): Ask students to say each picture aloud and listen to the beginning sound. Have them write the beginning letter on the line below the picture.
Blends (2): Ask students to say each picture aloud and listen to the beginning sound. Have them write the beginning blend on the line below the picture.
Alphabetical Order (3): Ask students to put the three letters in each group in alphabetical order.

Spectrum Reading Grade 1

Name_____

Where Are You?

1.

next to   over   above   below

in   over   under   below

2.

under   inside   around   below

outside   inside   under   below

3.

in   next to   around   above

in   beneath   under   next to

4.

down   up   sideways   under

down   up   around   near

Directions:

Using the Pictures (1-4): Have the student look at the pictures. Ask him or her to circle the word that describes where the objects are located.

Spectrum Reading Grade 1

84

Classify Me

1.	three	six	five	food
2.	orange	lemon	lime	ham
3.	penny	dime	nickel	dollar
4.	mouse	dog	bug	lion
5.	truck	car	boat	bus
6.	June	July	August	flag
7.	green	yellow	brown	tired
8.	stone	rock	brick	rug
9.	mom	dad	dog	sister
10.	funny	smile	laugh	mad

Directions:
Grouping Together (1-10): Have students read all four words in each line. Ask them to circle the three words that go together.

Alaska

Alaska is the largest state in America. It is the coldest state. It is two times as big as Texas and home to bears and eagles. If you lived in Alaska, you might see a blue glacier shining in the sun. Maybe you would see a bear, a moose, or even a pod of whales.

Juneau is the capital of Alaska. It is named after Joe Juneau. He went to Alaska in search of gold.

Many people in Alaska like to make and eat special ice cream. They mix berries with snow and seal oil.

Name_____

1. What might you see if you lived in Alaska?

_____ robins

_____ moose

_____ lions

2. Alaska is _____ as big as Texas.

two times   three times   ten times

3. What did Joe Juneau search for in Alaska? _____

bears   gold   diamonds

4. Which state is bigger?

_____ Alaska   _____ Texas

5. What is the special ice cream in Alaska made from?

_____ berries, cream, and seal oil

_____ snow, seal oil, and fish

_____ berries, snow, and seal oil

Thinking Further

1. Would you want to live in Alaska? Why or why not?

2. What are a few words that describe Alaska?

Directions:
Reading Skills—Comprehension and Facts and Details (1-5): Have students read the question and mark the correct answer.
Thinking Further (1-2): Have students read each question and then discuss their responses, or have them write down their thoughts on a separate sheet of paper.

New Mexico

New Mexico is a state full of red clay mountains. The capital of New Mexico is Santa Fe. It is the oldest capital city in America. This very old city was founded in 1610!

In Taos, New Mexico, you can see brown adobe houses. They are made from clay bricks baked in the sun.

In New Mexico, you might see bunches of red chili peppers. These are hung on strings outside houses. Sometimes, people leave the red chilies out all winter. They look beautiful in the white snow.

Name_____

Reading Skills

1. What might you see if you lived in New Mexico?

_____ bunches of chili peppers

_____ bunches of bananas

_____ bunches of green peppers

2. Santa Fe was founded in _____ 1610. _____ 1615. _____ 1910.

3. Adobe houses are made from _____ bricks.

_____ clay   _____ rock   _____ concrete

4. Why does Santa Fe have a star next to it on the map of New Mexico?

_____ The author lives there.

_____ It is the biggest city.

_____ It is the capital.

Thinking Further

1. Would you want to live in New Mexico? Why or why not?

2. What are a few words that describe New Mexico?

3. Were you surprised to find out that it snows in New Mexico? Why or why not?

Directions:
Reading Skills—Comprehension and Facts and Details (1-4): Have students read the question and mark the correct answer.
Thinking Further (1-3): Have students read each question and then discuss their responses, or have them write down their thoughts on a separate sheet of paper.

Oregon

Long, long ago, many people heard secrets about Oregon. They headed where the soil was good for farming. Many people wanted to travel across America to this state. They wanted to plant crops.

Traveling across America in a covered wagon was very dangerous. Travelers could go only in summer. They had to beat the coming cold weather. Many people on the Oregon Trail did not have enough food or fresh water. Many travelers died.

Today, you can visit Oregon by car, plane, or train. Maybe you'd want to visit Crater Lake National Park and see America's deepest lake.

Reading Skills

1. What might you see if you visited Oregon?

_____ the deepest lake   _____ the widest lake

_____ the coldest lake

2. Some people went to Oregon because it had _____ soil.

rich   poor   dirty

A **table of contents** tells you where to find things in a book. Use this table of contents to answer the questions.

Table of Contents

3. If you want to find out about Oregon's national parks, turn to page (5, 17).

4. If you want to find out where the city of Portland, Oregon is, turn to page (3, 25).

Thinking Further

1. Do you think there are farmers in Oregon? How do you know?

2. What are a few words that describe Oregon?

Directions:
Reading Skills—Comprehension and Facts and Details (1-4): Have students read the question and mark the correct answer.
Thinking Further (1-2): Have students read each question and then discuss their responses, or have them write down their thoughts on a separate sheet of paper.

Rhode Island

Rhode Island is the smallest state in America. It is nicknamed "Little Rhody."

If you visit, you might want to ride America's oldest merry-go-round in Watch Hill.

Maybe you'd want to take a ferry ride to Block Island. This is a tiny island off the coast. French pirates are said to have landed there. Captain Kidd's gold is thought to still be buried on the beautiful island.

Reading Skills

1. What island could you see in Rhode Island?

_____ Block Island

_____ Kidd Island

_____ Watch Island

2. Rhode Island is the _____ state.

smallest   largest   prettiest

3. Rhode Island has a nickname. It is

_____ "Little Rhody."

_____ "Bay State."

_____ "Pirate State."

4. If you wanted to go to Block Island, you could take a

_____ ferry.   _____ train.   _____ bus.

Thinking Further

1. Would you want to travel to Block Island? Why or why not?

2. Give Rhode Island another nickname.

3. Do you think that Captain Kidd's gold is still buried on Block Island? Why or why not?

Directions:
Reading Skills—Comprehension and Facts and Details (1-4): Have students read the question and mark the correct answer.
Thinking Further (1-3): Have students read each question and then discuss their responses, or have them write down their thoughts on a separate sheet of paper.

Vermont

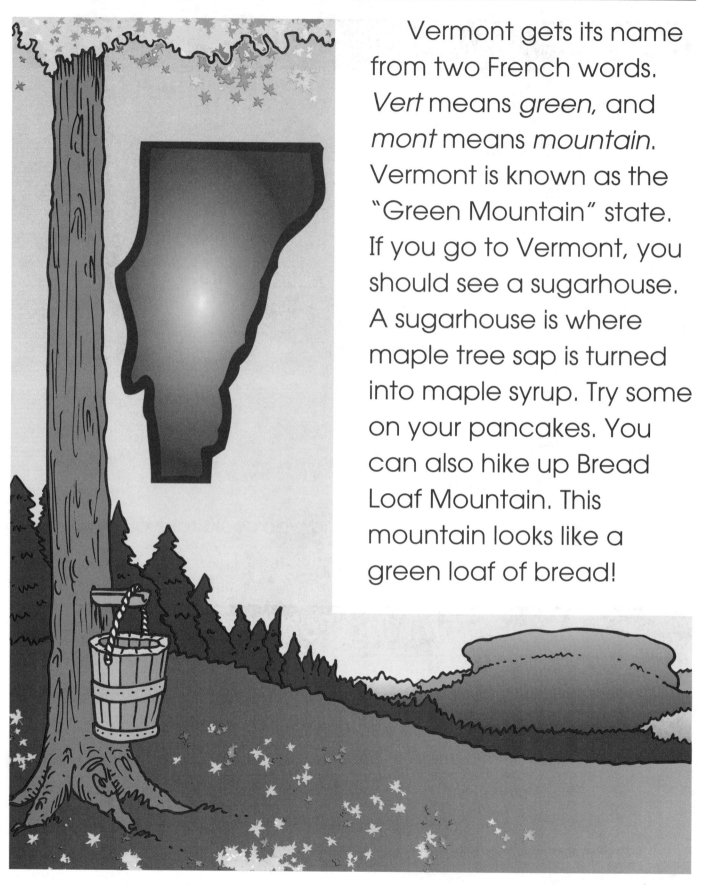

Vermont gets its name from two French words. *Vert* means *green,* and *mont* means *mountain.* Vermont is known as the "Green Mountain" state. If you go to Vermont, you should see a sugarhouse. A sugarhouse is where maple tree sap is turned into maple syrup. Try some on your pancakes. You can also hike up Bread Loaf Mountain. This mountain looks like a green loaf of bread!

Name_____

Reading Skills

1. What might you see if you live in Vermont?

_____ green mountains   _____ green rivers

_____ blue mountains   _____

2. You can climb

_____ Bread Loaf Mountain.   _____ Meatloaf Mountain.

_____ Butter Mountain.

3. Maple tree sap is turned into syrup. This happens in a

_____ milk house.   _____ sugarhouse.   _____ sap house.

4. What does Vermont's name mean?

_____ Tall Mountains   _____ Maple Mountains

_____ Green Mountains

5. Vermont's name comes from two _____ words.

_____ Spanish   _____ German   _____ French

Thinking Further

1. Would you want to live in Vermont? Why or why not?

2. What kind of tree is in the picture on page 94? How do you know?

Directions:
Reading Skills—Comprehension and Facts and Details (1-5): Have students read the question and mark the correct answer.
Thinking Further (1-2): Have students read each question and then discuss their responses, or have them write down their thoughts on a separate sheet of paper.

Kentucky

President Lincoln was born in Kentucky. He went to a log cabin school when he was a boy.

Kentucky is also the home of the Kentucky Derby. This is a famous horse race. Every May, horses race against each other.

In Kentucky, you can see the longest cave in the world. The cave has an underground river! You can take a boat trip down this dark river.

Reading Skills

1. What horse race takes place in Kentucky?

_____ Kentucky Derby

_____ Kentucky Doggie

_____ Kansas Derby

2. President _____ was born in Kentucky.

Lincoln   Kennedy   Washington

3. Kentucky has the longest _____ in the world.

cave   wave

4. In what month does the Kentucky Derby take place?

_____ May   _____ June   _____ July

5. What kind of school did Lincoln go to?

_____ a log cabin school   _____ a small stone schoolhouse

_____ a school for wealthy children

Thinking Further

1. Do you like horses? Would you want to see a race? Why or why not?

2. Give Kentucky a nickname.

Directions:
Reading Skills—Comprehension and Facts and Details (1-5): Have students read the question and mark the correct answer.
Thinking Further (1-2): Have students read each question and then discuss their responses, or have them write down their thoughts on a separate sheet of paper.

Connecticut

Connecticut is the birthplace of Noah Webster. Noah published the first American dictionary in 1806. Noah was born in West Hartford, Connecticut. He lived in a red saltbox house. In the winter, it was very cold. His family would sit around the huge brick fireplace in the kitchen. They would read by candlelight.

Today, Noah's old house is a museum. Many people visit each year. Spelling bees are held at his house. If you visit during a town spelling bee party, you can bob for apples and play with cornhusk dolls.

Webster's Dictionary

Name_____

1. Noah Webster grew up in

_____ West Hartford.

_____ East Hartford.

_____ West Hattyfields.

2. He lived in a _____ saltbox house.

black   brown   red

3. In what year did Noah publish his first dictionary?

_____ 1706   _____ 1806   _____ 1906

4. In Connecticut in the winter, it is

_____ very cold.

_____ damp.

_____ warm.

Thinking Further

1. Would you want to meet Noah Webster? Why or why not?

2. Would you want to write a dictionary?

3. Why do you think spelling bees are held at Noah's old house?

Directions:
Reading Skills—Comprehension and Facts and Details (1-4): Have students read the question and mark the correct answer.
Thinking Further (1-3): Have students read each question and then discuss their responses, or have them write down their thoughts on a separate sheet of paper.

New Hampshire

Robert Frost was a famous poet. He wrote many great poems. He lived in Derry, New Hampshire. Many of his poems are about nature. In his poems, he writes about fields of snow. He writes about leaves turning red in the fall. He writes about paths in the woods where people have traveled. Many of the ideas for his poems came from the land of New Hampshire.

Reading Skills

1. Robert Frost was a famous

_____ songwriter.

_____ poet.

_____ singer.

Poems

2. Many of his poems are about

_____ roses.   _____ buildings.   _____ nature.

3. What do you think Robert Frost would rather write a poem about?

_____ bikes   _____ trees   _____ trucks

4. Which of these statements is NOT true?

_____ Robert Frost lived in a town called Derry.

_____ Robert Frost wrote poems about fall leaves.

_____ No one knows where Robert got his ideas.

Thinking Further

1. Would you want to live in New Hampshire? Why or why not?

2. What would you like to write a poem about?

Directions:
Reading Skills—Comprehension and Facts and Details (1-4): Have students read the question and mark the correct answer.
Thinking Further (1-2): Have students read each question and then discuss their responses, or have them write down their thoughts on a separate sheet of paper.

Wisconsin

There are many dairy farmers in the state of Wisconsin. Dairy farmers make cheese, milk, and butter.

In fact, one of the largest hunks of cheese ever made came from here. "The Belle of Wisconsin" was a 40,060-pound cheddar cheese. This hunk of cheese was so big, it could make 300,000 grilled cheese sandwiches!

"The Belle of Wisconsin" toured America in a special car called the "Cheesemobile." It was sliced up and sold in 1989.

Reading Skills

1. There are many _____ in Wisconsin.

_____ teachers   _____ dairy farmers   _____ cowboys

2. Dairy farmers make

_____ orange juice.   _____ cheese.   _____ cookies.

3. Check the items below that are dairy products.

_____ milk   _____ apples   _____ butter

_____ cheese   _____ beef

4. What finally ended up happening to "The Belle of Wisconsin"?

_____ It got moldy.

_____ It was sliced and sold.

_____ It was turned into butter.

Thinking Further

1. Would you want to live in Wisconsin? Why or why not?

2. Would you want to tour America in the "Cheesemobile"? Why or why not?

3. What is your favorite dairy product?

Directions:
Reading Skills—Comprehension and Facts and Details (1-4): Have students read the question and mark the correct answer.
Thinking Further (1-3): Have students read each question and then discuss their responses, or have them write down their thoughts on a separate sheet of paper.

Montana

Montana is called "Big Sky Country." The big, blue sky seems to meet the land. One thing to visit here is Grasshopper Glacier. Millions of grasshoppers are frozen in the glacier ice for you to see.

Montana has more than 50 mountain ranges. Rocky Mountain goats call the rocks home. These white and furry goats can walk on sharp rocks. The goats are hard to see because they live so high up on the rocks.

Reading Skills

I. Montana is called

_____ "Big Time."

_____ "Big Sky Country."

_____ "Big Cow."

2. Grasshopper Glacier has _____ of frozen grasshoppers.

_____ a couple   _____ hundreds   _____ millions

3. Why are the Rocky Mountain goats hard to see?

_____ There are only a few of them.

_____ They blend in with the mountain.

_____ They live high up on the rocks.

4. In Montana, the sky seems to meet the

_____ land.   _____ sea.   _____ lake.

Thinking Further

I. Would you want to live in Montana? Why or why not?

2. Which would you want to see more, a grasshopper, glacier, or a Rocky Mountain goat? Explain why.

Directions:
Reading Skills—Comprehension and Facts and Details (1-4): Have students read the question and mark the correct answer.
Thinking Further (1-2): Have students read each question and then discuss their responses, or have them write down their thoughts on a separate sheet of paper.

Nevada

Nevada is the driest state in the United States. It has many human-made lakes. These lakes help bring water to the land. Two places you might want to visit here are a lake and a dam.

Lake Tahoe is a beautiful lake. It has snowy mountains all around it. It also has some of the clearest water.

Hoover Dam was named after the 31st president. Huge piles of cement were used to make the dam strong. The same amount of cement could be used to build a highway from New York City all the way to San Francisco!

Reading Skills

1. Nevada is the _____ state in the United States.

_____ rainiest

_____ driest

_____ hottest

2. Huge piles of cement were used to make Hoover Dam

_____ strong.   _____ gray.   _____ cold.

3. Who was Hoover Dam named after?

_____ the person who built it

_____ a president

_____ the governor of Nevada

4. The water in Lake Tahoe is

_____ clear.   _____ cloudy.   _____ shallow.

Thinking Further

1. Would you want to live in Nevada? Why or why not?

2. Would you want to help build a giant water dam? Why or why not?

Directions:
Reading Skills—Comprehension and Facts and Details (1-4): Have students read the question and mark the correct answer.
Thinking Further (1-2): Have students read each question and then discuss their responses, or have them write down their thoughts on a separate sheet of paper.

Texas

Texas is so big that it has two time zones. That means if you lived on one side of the state and Grandma lived on the other, you wouldn't want to call too late!

Big Bend National Park in Texas is a great place to visit. It has more birds and bats than any other U.S. park. If you visit, you might see horned toads, armadillos, and prairie dogs. All roads in the park end at the Rio Grande River.

Reading Skills

1. Texas is so big that it has _____ time zones.

_____ three

_____ two

_____ one

2. If you visit Big Bend National Park, what might you see?

_____ bats

_____ bears

_____ baboons

3. Why did the author write this article?

_____ to tell about armadillos

_____ to tell about the state of Texas

_____ to make the reader laugh

Thinking Further

1. Would you want to live in Texas? Why or why not?

2. If you visited, what animal would you most like to see?

Directions:
Reading Skills—Comprehension and Facts and Details (1-3): Have students read the question and mark the correct answer.
Thinking Further (1-2): Have students read each question and then discuss their responses, or have them write down their thoughts on a separate sheet of paper.

Hawaii

Hawaii is the 50th state. Over 100 islands make up Hawaii. New islands are still being made. These islands are made from volcanoes! Hawaii has black sand beaches also made from volcanoes.

The islands of Hawaii are in the middle of the Pacific Ocean. Some plants and animals found on Hawaii cannot be seen anywhere else.

If you visit Hawaii, you can visit a volcano. You can visit a black sand beach. When you get off the plane, people will say *aloha*. *Aloha* is how people welcome you in Hawaii. *Aloha* also means *love*.

Reading Skills

1. Over _____ islands make up Hawaii.

_____ one hundred

_____ two hundred

_____ three hundred

2. The word *aloha* means

_____ *like.*   _____ *pretty.*   _____ *love.*

3. Volcanoes make Hawaii's

_____ islands.   _____ weather.   _____ oceans.

4. Saying *aloha* is a way to _____ people.

_____ confuse

_____ welcome

_____ call

Thinking Further

1. Would you want to live in Hawaii? Why or why not?

2. Would you want to tour a volcano?

3. What is unusual about some of the plants and animals in Hawaii?

Directions:
Reading Skills—Comprehension and Facts and Details (1-4): Have students read the question and mark the correct answer.
Thinking Further (1-3): Have students read each question and then discuss their responses, or have them write down their thoughts on a separate sheet of paper.

Maryland

Maryland is known as "mini America." Here, you can see bays. You can see valleys. Maryland has beaches. Maryland has mountains, too.

If you visit this state, you can take a boat ride on the bay. You can visit the harbor where Francis Scott Key wrote a famous song. He was on a boat when he wrote the national anthem for America. Maryland has things for everybody to do.

Reading Skills

1. What might you see in Maryland?

_____ bays

_____ a rain forest

_____ the tallest mountain

2. Maryland has things to do for

_____ everybody.   _____ a few people.

3. Which of these is Maryland's nickname?

_____ "little America"   _____ "the Bay State"

_____ "mini America"

4. Francis Scott Key was on a _____ in a harbor when he wrote America's anthem.

_____ plane   _____ boat   _____ beach

Thinking Further

1. Would you like to live in Maryland? Why or why not?

2. What would you nickname Maryland?

3. How do you think Maryland got its nickname?

Directions:
Reading Skills—Comprehension and Facts and Details (1-4): Have students read the question and mark the correct answer.
Thinking Further (1-3): Have students read each question and then discuss their responses, or have them write down their thoughts on a separate sheet of paper.

Spectrum Reading Grade 1

113

California

California is the state with the most people in it. It is the third largest state.

This is a state where you can ski on a mountain. A few hours later, you can swim in the sea! In this state, you can see redwood forests and huge deserts.

This is a state where lots of movies are made. Many computer games are created here, too. This is a fun state to visit.

Name_____

Reading Skills

1. What might you see in California?

_____ movie making   _____ cornfields

_____ kangaroos

2. Why do so many people visit California?

_____ There are many pretty places to visit.

_____ There are lots of cars.

_____ There are lots of people.

3. Based on the article, you know that California is near

_____ the ocean.   _____ Florida.   _____ a big lake.

4. California is the largest state. Is this true or false?

_____ true   _____ false

Thinking Further

1. Would you like to live in California? Why or why not?

2. What would you nickname California?

3. Look at the picture near the top of this page. What does it help you understand about California?

Directions:
Reading Skills—Comprehension and Facts and Details (1-4): Have students read the question and mark the correct answer.
Thinking Further (1-3): Have students read each question and then discuss their responses, or have them write down their thoughts on a separate sheet of paper.

Spectrum Reading Grade 1

115

Florida

Come to Florida and see orange trees and beaches. You might even see some alligators.

Florida is also home to Cape Canaveral, where many spaceships are launched.

Florida often is very warm and sunny. Yet, in late summer, hurricanes can take place. Hurricanes are given names, such as Alex, Gloria, and Andrew.

Reading Skills

1. What might you see in Florida?

_____ polar bears

_____ alligators

_____ bears

2. What fruit is grown a lot in Florida?

_____ bananas   _____ apples   _____ oranges

3. In paragraph 2, what does the word *launched* mean?

_____ moved   _____ sent into the air   _____ stored

4. Based on the pictures, what kinds of trees do you think grow in Florida?

_____ palm trees   _____ redwood trees   _____ birch trees

Thinking Further

1. Would you like to live in Florida? Why or why not?

2. What nickname would you give Florida?

3. Tell what you know or have heard about hurricanes.

Directions:
Reading Skills—Comprehension and Facts and Details (1-4): Have students read the question and mark the correct answer.
Thinking Further (1-3): Have students read each question and then discuss their responses, or have them write down their thoughts on a separate sheet of paper.

New York

Visit the state of New York, and you will see rivers and busy cities. New York is the state where many people came first when moving to America long ago. Many new arrivals still make their homes in New York today.

New York City has more people than any other U.S. city. It has huge buildings. It has Broadway shows. It has yummy places to eat. New York City is also home to the Statue of Liberty.

Reading Skills

1. What might you see in New York?

_____ the Statue of Liberty _____ the Painting of Liberty

_____ the Statue of Freedom

2. Why might it be fun to visit New York City?

_____ There are a lot of fun things to do.

_____ It is sunny.

_____ There are a lot of roads.

3. Which of these best describes New York?

_____ a small city _____ a busy city _____ a country town

4. New York has more _____ than any other American city.

_____ statues _____ people _____ buses

Thinking Further

1. Would you like to visit New York? Why or why not?

2. What would you nickname New York?

3. When people are new to America, why do you think they go to New York?

Directions:
Reading Skills—Comprehension and Facts and Details (1-4): Have students read the question and mark the correct answer.
Thinking Further (1-3): Have students read each question and then discuss their responses, or have them write down their thoughts on a separate sheet of paper.

Pennsylvania

Pennsylvania was named after William Penn. Pennsylvania has lots of green valleys and farmland.

It is home to two big cities, Pittsburgh and Philadelphia. Philadelphia is where many important papers were signed for America. The Declaration of Independence was signed there. In Philadelphia, you can see the Liberty Bell, too.

Reading Skills

1. What might you see in Pennsylvania?

_____ the Liberty Bell

_____ the Statue of Liberty

_____ the Liberty Well

2. Philadelphia is a city where famous people signed

_____ baseball cards.   _____ important papers.   _____ art.

3. Who is Pennsylvania named after?

_____ William Penn

_____ Sylvia Penn

_____ Ben Franklin

4. Which of these is NOT a city in Pennsylvania?

_____ Pittsburgh   _____ Philadelphia   _____ Penn City

Thinking Further

1. Would you learn a lot by going to Philadelphia? Why or why not?

2. What are two words to describe Pennsylvania?

3. Tell what you know about the Declaration of Independence.

Directions:
Reading Skills—Comprehension and Facts and Details (1-4): Have students read the question and mark the correct answer.
Thinking Further (1-3): Have students read each question and then discuss their responses, or have them write down their thoughts on a separate sheet of paper.

South Dakota

Can you imagine seeing four huge faces carved into the side of a mountain? What if these faces were four of our presidents? Wow! Well, you can see this at Mount Rushmore in South Dakota.

You can also see the Badlands. Is this bad land? No! It is land full of gorges and mesas. A gorge is a narrow passage through a canyon. A mesa is a hill with a flat top. You can also see the Black Hills. These hills look dark from far away. Their name comes from a Lakota Indian word.

Name_____

1. Mount Rushmore has _____ faces carved out of stone.

_____ three

_____ two

_____ four

2. The Badlands are

_____ bad.   _____ good.   _____ filled with gorges.

3. Whose faces are carved in Mount Rushmore?

_____ hikers   _____ presidents   _____ athletes

4. What is a mesa?

_____ a desert

_____ a lake

_____ a hill with a flat top

Thinking Further

1. Would you want to see Mount Rushmore? Why or why not?

2. Do you think it would be hard to carve people's heads out of stone? Why or why not?

Directions:
Reading Skills—Comprehension and Facts and Details (1-4): Have students read the question and mark the correct answer.
Thinking Further (1-2): Have students read each question and then discuss their responses, or have them write down their thoughts on a separate sheet of paper.

Virginia

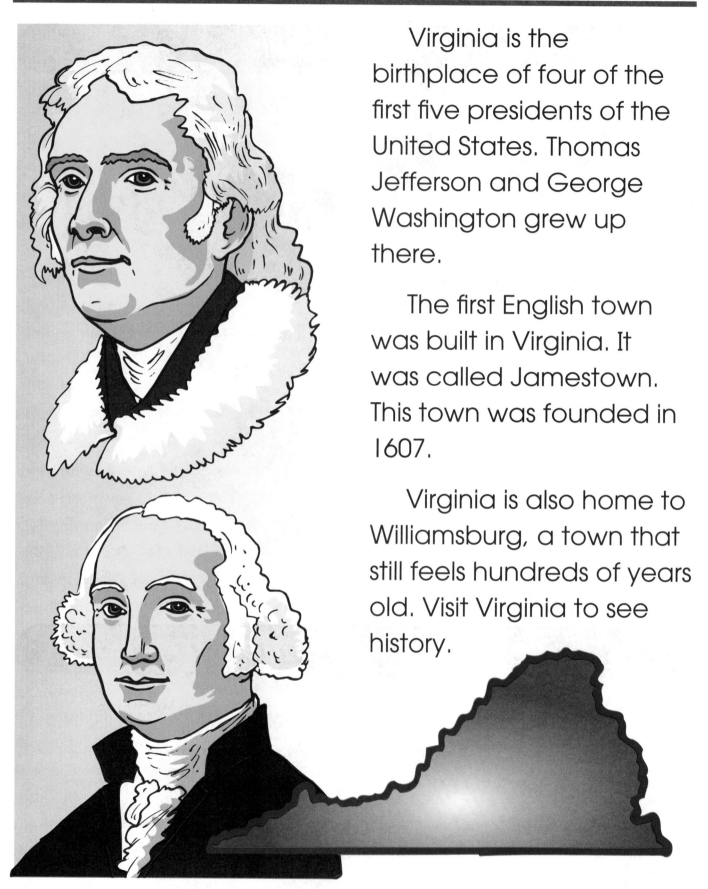

Virginia is the birthplace of four of the first five presidents of the United States. Thomas Jefferson and George Washington grew up there.

The first English town was built in Virginia. It was called Jamestown. This town was founded in 1607.

Virginia is also home to Williamsburg, a town that still feels hundreds of years old. Visit Virginia to see history.

Name_____

Reading Skills

1. What president was born in Virginia?

_____ George Washington

_____ George Bush

_____ King George

2. What was the name of the first English town?

_____ Jamestown

_____ Jimstown

3. The first English _____ was built in Virginia.

park   town   barn

Thinking Further

1. Would you like to visit Virginia? Why or why not?

2. What do you think you might see in an old fashioned town like Williamsburg?

3. In the second paragraph, it says that Jamestown was founded in 1607. What do you think *founded* means?

Directions:
Reading Skills—Comprehension and Facts and Details (1-3): Have students read the question and mark the correct answer.
Thinking Further (1-3): Have students read each question and then discuss their responses, or have them write down their thoughts on a separate sheet of paper.

Minnesota

It is freezing cold! Winters in Minnesota can be so cold that wet hair turns to ice. Bundle up!

The summers are warm. You can go fishing or boating. You can swim in many of the state's thousands of lakes.

Minnesota is also home to two big cities. These cities are next to each other. They are Minneapolis and St. Paul. These two cities are known as the "Twin Cities."

Reading Skills

1. Winters in Minnesota can be so cold that wet hair turns to

_____ snow.

_____ ice.

_____ dark.

2. Where might you go swimming in Minnesota?

_____ lakes   _____ parks   _____ oceans

3. The cities of Minneapolis and St. Paul are known as the

_____ "Double Cities."   _____ "Twin Cities."

_____ "Chilly Cities."

4. Fishing and boating are fun to do in Minnesota during the

_____ winter.   _____ summer.

Thinking Further

1. Would you want to visit Minnesota? Why or why not?

2. What are two words that describe Minnesota?

3. If you lived in Minnesota, would you like summer or winter better? Why?

Directions:
Reading Skills—Comprehension and Facts and Details (1-4): Have students read the question and mark the correct answer.
Thinking Further (1-3): Have students read each question and then discuss their responses, or have them write down their thoughts on a separate sheet of paper.

Colorado

Denver is the capital of Colorado. It is also a mile up in the sky. It is called the "Mile High City."

Colorado is a state in the Rocky Mountains. Many people love to visit and go skiing. Some people bike the mountain paths. Other people like to ride rafts in the wild rivers there.

☆
DENVER

Name_____

Reading Skills

1. The city of Denver is _____ in the sky.

_____ low

_____ high

_____ blue

2. Some people come to this state to

_____ ski.   _____ surf.   _____ see fish.

3. What is the capital of Colorado?

_____ Rocky Mountain

_____ Mile City

_____ Denver

Thinking Further

1. Would you like to ski, bike, or raft in Colorado? Why?

2. What are two words to describe Colorado?

3. What does the red star by Denver on the map mean?

Directions:
Reading Skills—Comprehension and Facts and Details (1-3): Have students read the question and mark the correct answer.
Thinking Further (1-3): Have students read each question and then discuss their responses, or have them write down their thoughts on a separate sheet of paper.

Arizona

Arizona is a great place. It is home to the Grand Canyon. This canyon is a wonder of the world. Millions of people visit it each year. They come to see its shapes and colors. Parts of the Grand Canyon are billions of years old!

If you visit the Grand Canyon, you might see fossils. You can camp overnight. Maybe you would want to ride a mule. Some people even raft down the river. Other people like to see the rocks from above. They take a plane ride and see the canyon from high in the sky.

Reading Skills

1. Why do people come to see the Grand Canyon?

_____ the sunshine

_____ the shapes of the rocks

_____ the food

2. What are some things you can do at the Grand Canyon?

_____ look for fossils

_____ take a train ride

_____ make soap

3. How many people visit the Grand Canyon every year?

_____ millions   _____ thousands   _____ hundreds

Thinking Further

1. Would you like to see the Grand Canyon? Why or why not?

2. What are two words to describe the Grand Canyon?

3. How does the author feel about Arizona? How do you know?

Directions:
Reading Skills—Comprehension and Facts and Details (1-3): Have students read the question and mark the correct answer.
Thinking Further (1-3): Have students read each question and then discuss their responses, or have them write down their thoughts on a separate sheet of paper.

Words to Know

1.
duck
dog
did

2.
for
fish
from

3.
grass
green
go

4.
bowl
bee
big

5.
call
can't
cold

6.
water
wet
won't

7.
pond
put
play

8.
foot
farm
for

9.
can
class
corn

10.
hop
hat
him

11.
road
run
red

12.
sun
son
sit

13.
pull
push
pail

14.
soft
set
says

15.
sleep
slip
sled

Directions:
Recognizing Familiar Words (1-15): Ask students to say the name of each picture and then circle the word that best describes the picture.

Words to Know

1.  snap
snail
snore

2. has
hand
her

3. pine
penny
pinch

4.  was
wing
wish

5.  fox
for
from

6.  dinner
dime
don't

7.  am
apple
ape

8.  want
wish
will

9. whale
wink
what

10.  friend
feet
from

11. fly
fry
fun

12.  sun
star
skip

13.  kit
kite
kiss

14.  gift
give
get

15. string
step
skunk

Directions:
Recognizing Familiar Words (1-15): Ask students to say the name of each picture and then circle the word that best describes the picture.

Contractions

can't   didn't
won't   let's
don't   that's
isn't   I'll
wasn't

1. do not _____

2. let us _____

3. will not _____

4. was not _____

5. is not _____

6. that is _____

7. can not _____

8. did not _____

9. I will _____

Directions:

Introducing Contractions (1-9): Explain the concept of contractions to students. Ask them to read aloud the contractions at the top of the page. Then, ask students to read the numbered pair of words. Next, have students write the correct contraction for the two words.

Lost Letters

1. Why does Little Duck want to fly?

   He wants to see the blue s____y.

2. How can he fly?

   With his w____ngs.

3. Do boys and girls have wings?

   N____t that I can se____.

4. Do fish have wings?

   N____, but they have f____ns.

5. Can Little Duck dive?

   Yes, he can d____ve.

Directions:
Missing Letters (1-5): Have students read each sentence and fill in the missing letters.

Lost Letters

1. What animal did Carolyn pick?

She picked a k____tten.

2. How did the kitten feel?

The new kitten felt s____ft.

3. What kind of pets do most people have?

Most people have c____ts or d____gs.

4. Do some people have different pets?

Max has a pet fr____g and a pet t____rtle.

5. Would a tiger make a good pet?

No, a tiger wo____'t make a good pet.

Name

Words to Know

1.  hall
home
hop

2. bear
bee
big

3. pat
pet
pit

4. green
great
good

5. bench
boat
belt

6. like
love
log

7. to
two
toe

8. bend
back
bath

9. big
bring
bow

10. bars
bug
birds

11. call
can't
can

12. land
lick
lip

13. can
cage
call

14.  play
pan
pin

15. ran
run
rock

Directions:
Recognizing Familiar Words (1-15): Ask students to say the name of each picture and then circle the word that best describes the picture.

Spectrum Reading Grade 1

137

Answer Key

Beautiful Beginnings

I.

b	b	n

2.

d	d	w

3.

I	3	2

3

Beautiful Beginnings

I.
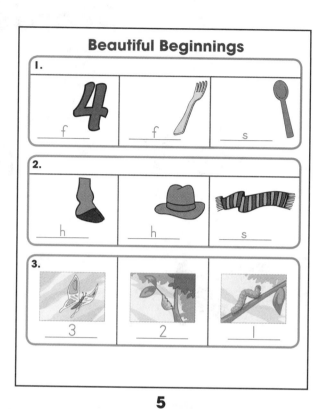

f	f	s

2.

h	h	s

3.

3	2	I

5

Beautiful Beginnings

I.

j	j	h

2.

l	l	t

3.

3	I	2

7

Beautiful Beginnings

I.

h	s	m

2.

n	n	m

3.

ten ——— clap
snap ——— dime
chime ——— pen
four ——— score

9

Answer Key

Beautiful Beginnings

1. d   c   k
2. r   b   m
3. 1   3   2

11

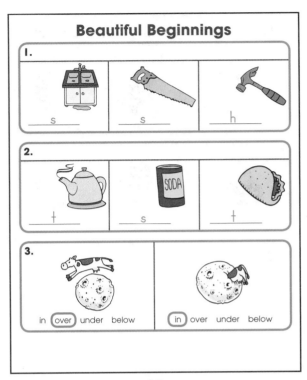

Beautiful Beginnings

1. s   s   h
2. t   s   t
3. in (over) under below   (in) over under below

13

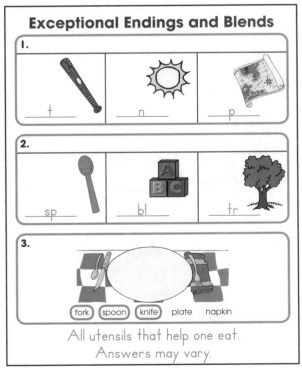

Exceptional Endings and Blends

1. t   n   p
2. sp   bl   tr
3. (fork) (spoon) (knife) plate napkin

All utensils that help one eat.
Answers may vary.

15

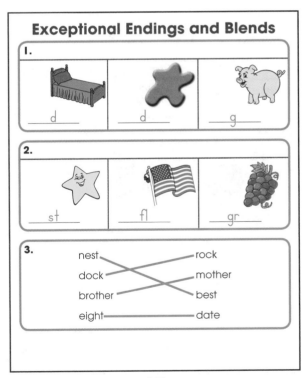

Exceptional Endings and Blends

1. d   d   g
2. st   fl   gr
3.
nest — mother
dock — best
brother — rock
eight — date

17

Answer Key

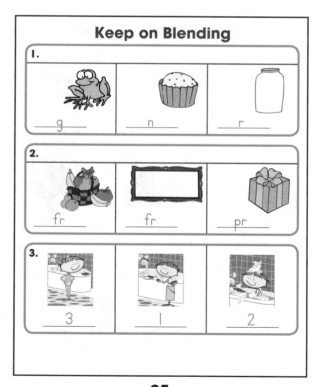

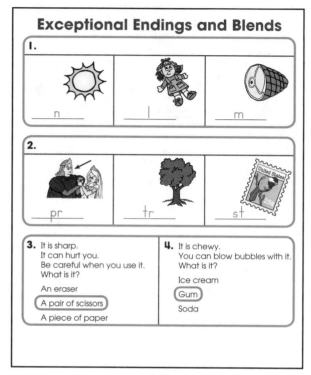 is page 19, Exceptional Endings and Blends
 is page 21, Endless Endings and page 25, Keep on Blending
 is page 23, More Endings

---

Exceptional Endings and Blends (page 19)

1. n | l | m

2. pr | tr | st

3. It is sharp.
It can hurt you.
Be careful when you use it.
What is it?
An eraser
(A pair of scissors)
A piece of paper

4. It is chewy.
You can blow bubbles with it.
What is it?
Ice cream
(Gum)
Soda

19

Endless Endings (page 21)

1. n | d | r

2. school | student | teacher | doctor
3. bird | frog | human | dog
4. circle | two | eight | six

5. There are four birds.
There are five birds.

6. There are 5 – 2 toads.
There are 1 + 3 toads.

21

More Endings (page 23)

1. n | s | t

2. tr | fr | gr

3. Write a sentence that includes one of the pictures above in #2.
Answers will vary. Example:
My grandfather has freckles.

23

Keep on Blending (page 25)

1. g | n | r

2. fr | fr | pr

3. 3 | 1 | 2

25

Answer Key

Is the End in Sight?

1.

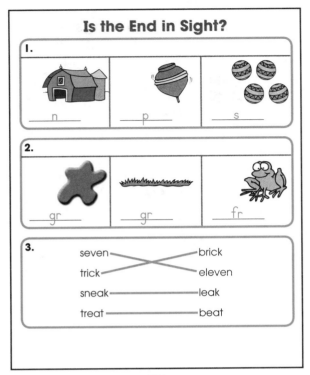

n	p	s

2.

gr	gr	fr

3.

seven ⟋⟍ brick
trick ⟋⟍ eleven
sneak ——— leak
treat ——— beat

27

Vowels and Digraphs

1.

a	e	i

2.

ch	ch	

3.

nickel, dime

29

Vowels

1.

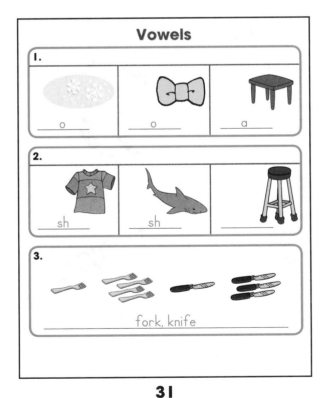

o	o	a

2.

sh	sh	

3.

fork, knife

31

Dynamite Digraphs

1.

th	th	

2.

a	u	o

3.

Answers will vary.

33

Answer Key

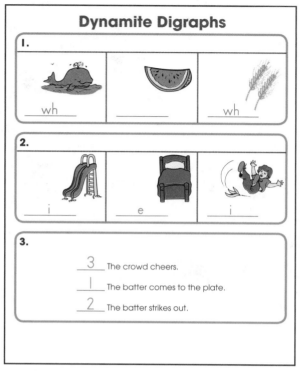

Dynamite Digraphs

1.

wh___	_____	wh___

2.

___i___	___e___	___i___

3.

   __3__ The crowd cheers.

   __1__ The batter comes to the plate.

   __2__ The batter strikes out.

35

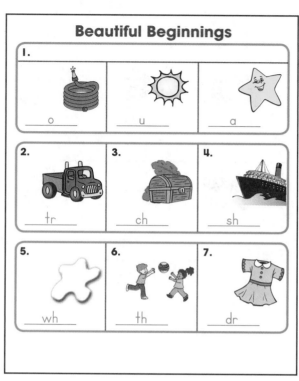

Beautiful Beginnings

1.

___o	___u	___a

2.	**3.**	**4.**
tr___	ch___	sh___

5.	**6.**	**7.**
wh___	th___	dr___

37

Go Short or Go Long: Aa

1. ate ___long___
2. at ___short___
3. ape ___long___
4. act ___short___
5. ant ___short___
6. age ___long___
7. rake ___long___
8. ray ___long___
9. able ___long___
10. rat ___short___
11. rack ___short___
12. rate ___long___
13. Andy ___short___
14. Alex ___short___
15. Abe ___long___

39

Go Short or Go Long: Ee

1. pen ___short___
2. pencil ___short___
3. plea ___long___
4. pea ___long___
5. glee ___long___
6. green ___long___
7. tea ___long___
8. ten ___short___
9. teen ___long___
10. hen ___short___
11. fence ___short___
12. bee ___long___
13. be ___long___
14. bend ___short___
15. Ben ___short___

41

Answer Key

Go Short or Go Long: Ii

1. pie _long_
2. pin _short_
3. pine _long_
4. pink _short_
5. pit _short_
6. tin _short_
7. time _long_
8. tiny _long_
9. tick _short_
10. Tim _short_
11. die _long_
12. dim _short_
13. diet _long_
14. dine _long_
15. dinner _short_

43

Go Short or Go Long: Oo

1. pot _short_
2. spot _short_
3. snow _long_
4. not _short_
5. oat _long_
6. on _short_
7. box _short_
8. mop _short_
9. rope _long_
10. Oliver _short_
11. show _long_
12. shop _short_
13. hot _short_
14. stop _short_
15. slope _long_

45

Go Short or Go Long: Uu

1. under _short_
2. cube _long_
3. umbrella _short_
4. cut _short_
5. cute _long_
6. butter _short_
7. yummy _short_
8. mule _long_
9. club _short_
10. duck _short_
11. dune _long_
12. tuck _short_
13. tune _long_
14. run _short_
15. funny _short_

47

Big Time Rhyme

1. funny
2. honey
3. duck
4. stop
5. ton
6. snow
7. bear
8. spring
9. fall
10. tell
11. tear

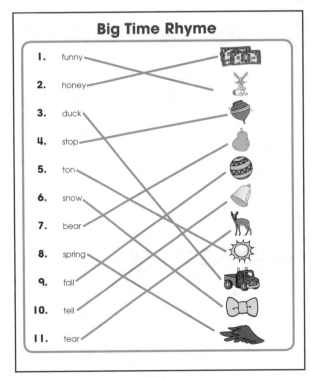

48

Answer Key

Classified Information

1. (sad) (glad) (mad) cage
2. (five) (alive) (nine) thirteen
3. (boat) (don't) (won't) did
4. (wheat) (seat) (beat) cat
5. (pie) (pine) pin (spine)
6. jump (true) (cube) (June)
7. (oat) (coat) spot (moat)
8. (glee) (green) gem (greet)
9. (hen) (ten) (tent) teen
10. (ray) rat (rake) (rate)

49

Reading Skills

1. This story is about
   - _X_ Carolyn wanting a pet.
   - _____ Carolyn wanting a toy.
   - _____ how Carolyn is sad.
2. Carolyn has posters on the walls of
   - _____ horses.   _X_ puppies.   _____ flowers.
3. The **setting** is where a story takes place. What is the setting for this story?
   - _____ Carolyn's kitchen
   - _____ Carolyn's living room
   - _X_ Carolyn's bedroom
4. In the picture on page 50, how does Carolyn look?
   - _X_ sad   _____ happy   _____ bored

Thinking Further and Predicting Outcomes

1. Do you think Carolyn will get a real pet or more teddy bears? How come?

51

Reading Skills

1. This story is about
   - _____ Carolyn hearing about how pets are bad.
   - _X_ Carolyn hearing about how pets take work.
   - _____ Carolyn hearing about how dirty pets are.
2. Carolyn's aunt's name is _____ Lucinda. _____ Lucy. _X_ Linda.
3. What does Mrs. Jones want Carolyn to do?
   - _____ get a new stuffed animal
   - _X_ think about whether she is ready for a pet
   - _____ forget about getting a pet
4. Carolyn comes to talk to Mom while Mom is
   - _X_ reading.   _____ working.   _____ napping.

Thinking Further and Predicting Outcomes

1. Do you think Carolyn would take good care of a pet? How come?
2. Do you think Carolyn's mother will help her get a pet? How come?

53

Reading Skills

1. In this story,
   - _____ Carolyn thinks that she will have lots of time to care for a pet.
   - _X_ Carolyn thinks she might not have enough time for a pet.
   - _____ Carolyn decides she doesn't want a pet.
2. Carolyn talks to her
   - _____ aunt.   _X_ teddy bear.   _____ posters.
3. In this story, Carolyn feels
   - _____ excited.   _X_ worried.   _____ mad.
4. Which of these is NOT something that takes up Carolyn's time?
   - _X_ soccer practice _____ homework _____ a school play

Thinking Further and Predicting Outcomes

1. Do you think Carolyn can handle both a pet and school work?
2. Do you think if Carolyn gets a pet, she will take good care of it?
3. If Carolyn had a pet, do you think she would talk to it? Why or why not?

55

Answer Key

Reading Skills

1. In this story,

_____ Carolyn's dad tells her she can't have a pet.

__X__ Carolyn's dad talks about other types of pets.

_____ Carolyn's dad says he will get her a dog.

2. Carolyn's dad mentions a possible pet. It is a

__X__ turtle.   _____ bunny.   _____ pony.

3. Who is the main character in the story?

_____ Mrs. Jones

_____ Mr. Jones

__X__ Carolyn

4. Carolyn's mom and dad _____ about pets being a lot of work.

__X__ agree   _____ do not agree

Thinking Further and Predicting Outcomes

1. Do you think Carolyn would enjoy a pet turtle?

2. Do you think Carolyn's dad knows why she wants a pet? Why or why not?

57

Reading Skills

1. In this story,

__X__ Carolyn explains how she would take care of her new pet.

_____ Carolyn says she is sad.

_____ Carolyn talks about her friends at school.

2. The pet will be named _____ Prince. __X__ Promise. _____ Misty.

3. This story takes place

__X__ in the morning. _____ at lunchtime. _____ before bed.

4. When will Carolyn's parents tell her their answer?

__X__ tomorrow   _____ Monday   _____ after lunch

5. Who is telling the story?

_____ Carolyn   __X__ the author   _____ Carolyn's mom

Thinking Further and Predicting Outcomes

1. Do you think Carolyn has explained herself well? How do you know?

2. Do you think Carolyn's parents like her plan? Why or why not?

59

Reading Skills

1. This story is about

__X__ Carolyn waking up early to find out if she will get a pet.

_____ Carolyn waking up early to go to school.

_____ Carolyn sleeping because she is so tired.

2. Carolyn's last name is __X__ Jones. _____ Promise. _____ Linda.

3. Which of these is NOT something Carolyn will do for her pet?

_____ brush its fur

_____ love it

__X__ clip its nails

4. Look at the picture on page 60. Carolyn looks

__X__ excited.   _____ sneaky.   _____ grumpy.

Thinking Further and Predicting Outcomes

1. What will the decision be?

2. Why do people love pets?

3. How do you think Carolyn feels as she comes running down the stairs?

61

Reading Skills

1. This story is about

__X__ Carolyn finding out that she will get a pet.

_____ Carolyn finding out that she will not get a pet.

_____ Carolyn finding out she's late for school.

2. Carolyn hugged her _____ mother. _____ father. __X__ parents.

3. Carolyn's dad has a big smile on his face when he has something _____ to say.

_____ strange   __X__ good   _____ bad

4. What is the setting for this story?

__X__ the kitchen

_____ the den

_____ Carolyn's bedroom

Thinking Further and Predicting Outcomes

1. Where will the Jones family get their pet?

2. Do you think Carolyn's parents made the right decision? How come?

63

Answer Key

Reading Skills

1. This story is about

__X__ Carolyn telling her friends about getting a pet.

_____ Carolyn telling her friends about her school project.

_____ Carolyn's visit to the pound.

2. What was the name of Carolyn's friend who asked about her new pet? His name is

__X__ Freddy.   _____ Eddie.   _____ Betty.

3. Carolyn tells Freddy that she would like to get a puppy or

_____ an alligator.

__X__ a kitten.

_____ a goldfish.

4. Where will the Jones family go to get a pet?

__X__ the pound   _____ the pet store   _____ a farm

Thinking Further and Predicting Outcomes

1. Do you think Carolyn will show her pet to her classmates? Why or why not?

65

Reading Skills

1. This story is about

__X__ Carolyn learning about the pound.

_____ Carolyn wanting to go to the pet store.

_____ Carolyn changing her mind about getting a pet.

2. Mrs. Jones and Carolyn will go to the

__X__ pound.   _____ pet store.   _____ zoo.

3. In the picture above, what is Carolyn thinking about?

_____ a stuffed dog   _____ a teddy bear   __X__ a real dog

4. Which kind of animal will Carolyn and her mom NOT see at the pound?

_____ cats   _____ rabbits   __X__ chickens

Thinking Further and Predicting Outcomes

1. Do you think it's a good idea to go to the pound for a pet? Why or why not?

2. What will Carolyn do when she chooses her pet?

67

Reading Skills

1. This story is about

__X__ Carolyn seeing all sorts of animals at the pound.

_____ Carolyn feeling scared.

_____ Carolyn playing with a lizard.

2. Carolyn pets a kitten that is

_____ eating.   __X__ sleeping.   _____ drinking.

3. How did the fat cat's tongue feel on Carolyn's hand?

__X__ scratchy   _____ soft   _____ slimy

4. There was only one kind of animal at the pound.

_____ true

__X__ false

Thinking Further and Predicting Outcomes

1. Will Carolyn choose a pet after all? How do you know?

2. Will Carolyn get more than one pet? How do you know?

3. What kinds of words are used to describe the dogs?

fat, skinny, furry

69

Reading Skills

1. This story is about

__X__ Carolyn realizing that taking care of only one pet is still a good thing.

_____ Carolyn realizing that she should take five pets.

_____ Carolyn leaving the pound with no pets.

2. The pets are living in __X__ cages. _____ houses. _____ boxes.

3. The pound needs more

_____ cats.   _____ dogs.   __X__ workers.

4. Carolyn wishes that all the animals had someone to _____ them.

_____ wash   __X__ love   _____ name

Thinking Further and Predicting Outcomes

1. Do you think Carolyn will feel better about taking only one pet? How come?

2. Do you think Carolyn is a caring person? Why or why not?

3. The next time Carolyn gets a pet, do you think she will go to the pound again? Why or why not?

71

Answer Key

Reading Skills

I. This story is about

  __X__ Carolyn choosing a kitten.

  _____ Carolyn choosing a puppy.

  _____ Carolyn choosing two puppies.

2. What color is the kitten? __X__ white _____ black _____ brown

3. Which sentence is true?

  _____ Mom had to choose for Carolyn.

  __X__ Carolyn chose the sleeping kitten.

  _____ Carolyn decided to get a kitten and a puppy.

4. Carolyn thinks the kitten looks like

  __X__ a baby cloud. _____ a snowball. _____ a cotton ball.

Thinking Further and Predicting Outcomes

I. Do you think Carolyn will always take good care of her kitten? How come?

2. Do you think Carolyn will be happy with her new pet? Why or why not?

73

Reading Skills

I. In this story,

  __X__ Carolyn realizes she cannot have her kitten until tomorrow.

  _____ Carolyn learns that the kitten belongs to someone.

  _____ Carolyn learns that the kitten is 3 years old.

2. The kitten is a __X__ boy. _____ girl.

3. Before the kitten can come home with Carolyn, it needs to have its _____.

  _____ food __X__ shots _____ training

4. Mrs. Jones thinks that the kitten is

  _____ too little. _____ too wild. __X__ beautiful.

Thinking Further and Predicting Outcomes

I. Do you think Carolyn will be upset that she can't have the kitten right away? How come?

2. Do you think Carolyn will be nervous for the kitten because he needs shots? How come?

75

Reading Skills

I. This story is about

  __X__ Carolyn getting a gift from her dad.

  _____ Carolyn learning to study.

  _____ Carolyn playing with Promise.

2. The new kitten is like a

  __X__ cotton ball. _____ paper. _____ snow.

3. Carolyn's dad asks if they should call the kitten Cloudy or

  _____ Buttons. _____ Snowy. __X__ Mr. Cotton.

4. What does Mr. Jones buy as a gift for Promise Jones?

  __X__ a cat bed _____ a scratching post _____ litter

Thinking Further and Predicting Outcomes

I. Do you think Carolyn makes the right decision about keeping Promise's name the same? Why?

2. Do you like soft things? Why?

3. If you got a kitten, what would you name it?

77

Reading Skills

I. This story is about

  __X__ Carolyn promising to care for her cat.

  _____ Carolyn eating dinner with her cat.

  _____ Carolyn having a party with her parents.

2. Carolyn plays with her new pet in the

  _____ bedroom. __X__ family room. _____ kitchen.

3. How do you think Promise Jones felt?

  __X__ shy _____ sad _____ lazy

4. What is Carolyn's promise to her new kitten?

  _____ She will play with him every day.

  _____ She will not get any more pets.

  __X__ He has found a home.

Thinking Further and Predicting Outcomes

I. Do you think Carolyn will ever want another pet? Why?

2. Would you want somebody like Carolyn as your friend? Why or why not?

79

Answer Key

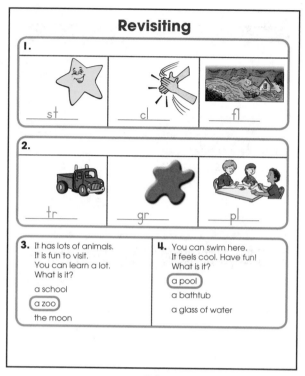

Revisiting

I.
st | cl | fl

2.
tr | gr | pl

3. It has lots of animals.
It is fun to visit.
You can learn a lot.
What is it?

a school
(a zoo)
the moon

4. You can swim here.
It feels cool. Have fun!
What is it?

(a pool)
a bathtub
a glass of water

80

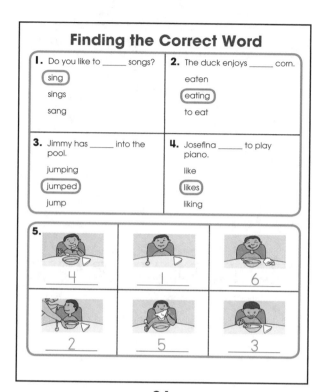

Finding the Correct Word

I. Do you like to _____ songs?
(sing)
sings
sang

2. The duck enjoys _____ corn.
eaten
(eating)
to eat

3. Jimmy has _____ into the pool.
jumping
(jumped)
jump

4. Josefina _____ to play piano.
like
(likes)
liking

5.
4 | 1 | 6
2 | 5 | 3

81

Blends Review

I. st___l
2. sn___p
3. gr___s
4. st___k
5. st___r
6. sl___d
7. tr___n
8. sc___f

82

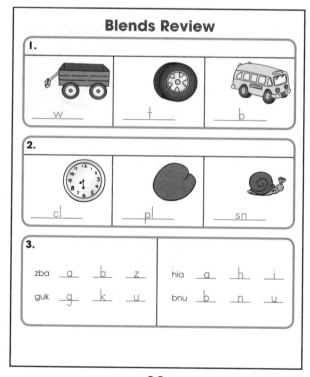

Blends Review

I.
w | t | b

2.
cl | pl | sn

3.
zba a b z | hia a h i
guk g k u | bnu b n u

83

Answer Key

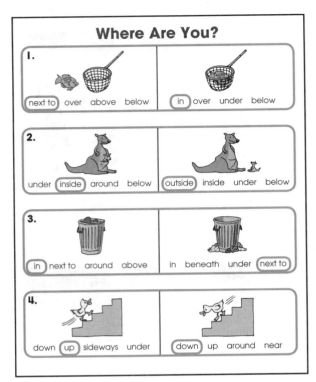

Where Are You?

1.
- next to / over / above / below
- in / over / under / below

2.
- under / inside / around / below
- outside / inside / under / below

3.
- in / next to / around / above
- in / beneath / under / next to

4.
- down / up / sideways / under
- down / up / around / near

84

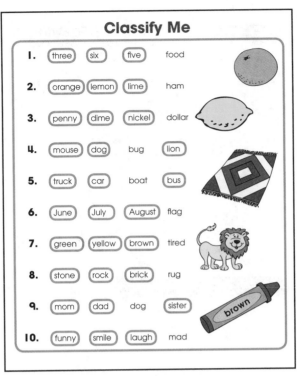

Classify Me

1. three   six   five   food
2. orange   lemon   lime   ham
3. penny   dime   nickel   dollar
4. mouse   dog   bug   lion
5. truck   car   boat   bus
6. June   July   August   flag
7. green   yellow   brown   tired
8. stone   rock   brick   rug
9. mom   dad   dog   sister
10. funny   smile   laugh   mad

85

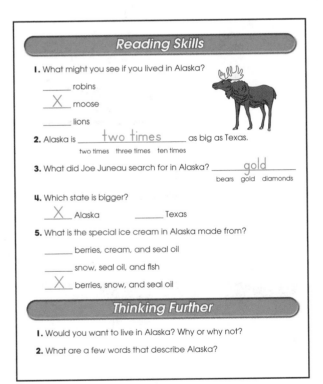

Reading Skills

1. What might you see if you lived in Alaska?
   - _____ robins
   - __X__ moose
   - _____ lions
2. Alaska is __two times__ as big as Texas.
   two times   three times   ten times
3. What did Joe Juneau search for in Alaska? __gold__
   bears   gold   diamonds
4. Which state is bigger?
   - __X__ Alaska
   - _____ Texas
5. What is the special ice cream in Alaska made from?
   - _____ berries, cream, and seal oil
   - _____ snow, seal oil, and fish
   - __X__ berries, snow, and seal oil

Thinking Further

1. Would you want to live in Alaska? Why or why not?
2. What are a few words that describe Alaska?

87

Reading Skills

1. What might you see if you lived in New Mexico?
   - __X__ bunches of chili peppers
   - _____ bunches of bananas
   - _____ bunches of green peppers
2. Santa Fe was founded in __X__ 1610. _____ 1615. _____ 1910.
3. Adobe houses are made from _____ bricks.
   - __X__ clay
   - _____ rock
   - _____ concrete
4. Why does Santa Fe have a star next to it on the map of New Mexico?
   - _____ The author lives there.
   - _____ It is the biggest city.
   - __X__ It is the capital.

Thinking Further

1. Would you want to live in New Mexico? Why or why not?
2. What are a few words that describe New Mexico?
3. Were you surprised to find out that it snows in New Mexico? Why or why not?

89

Answer Key

Reading Skills

1. What might you see if you visited Oregon?

___X___ the deepest lake   _____ the widest lake

_____ the coldest lake

2. Some people went to Oregon because it had ___rich___ soil.

     rich   poor   dirty

A **table of contents** tells you where to find things in a book. Use this table of contents to answer the questions.

Table of Contents

Map of Oregon 3
The Oregon Trail 5
Oregon's Natural Beauty 17
Famous People of Oregon 25
Oregon Today 33

3. If you want to find out about Oregon's national parks, turn to page (5, (17)).

4. If you want to find out where the city of Portland, Oregon is, turn to page ((3), 25).

Thinking Further

1. Do you think there are farmers in Oregon? How do you know?

2. What are a few words that describe Oregon?

91

Reading Skills

1. What island could you see in Rhode Island?

___X___ Block Island

_____ Kidd Island

_____ Watch Island

2. Rhode Island is the ___smallest___ state.

     smallest   largest   prettiest

3. Rhode Island has a nickname. It is

___X___ "Little Rhody."

_____ "Bay State."

_____ "Pirate State."

4. If you wanted to go to Block Island, you could take a

___X___ ferry.   _____ train.   _____ bus.

Thinking Further

1. Would you want to travel to Block Island? Why or why not?

2. Give Rhode Island another nickname.

3. Do you think that Captain Kidd's gold is still buried on Block Island? Why or why not?

93

Reading Skills

1. What might you see if you live in Vermont?

___X___ green mountains   _____ green rivers

_____ blue mountains

2. You can climb

___X___ Bread Loaf Mountain.   _____ Meatloaf Mountain.

_____ Butter Mountain.

3. Maple tree sap is turned into syrup. This happens in a

_____ milk house.   ___X___ sugarhouse.   _____ sap house.

4. What does Vermont's name mean?

_____ Tall Mountains   _____ Maple Mountains

___X___ Green Mountains

5. Vermont's name comes from two _____ words.

_____ Spanish   _____ German   ___X___ French

Thinking Further

1. Would you want to live in Vermont? Why or why not?

2. What kind of tree is in the picture on page 94? How do you know?

maple; It is being tapped for syrup.

95

Reading Skills

1. What horse race takes place in Kentucky?

___X___ Kentucky Derby

_____ Kentucky Doggie

_____ Kansas Derby

2. President ___Lincoln___ was born in Kentucky.

     Lincoln   Kennedy   Washington

3. Kentucky has the longest ___cave___ in the world.

     cave   wave

4. In what month does the Kentucky Derby take place?

___X___ May   _____ June   _____ July

5. What kind of school did Lincoln go to?

___X___ a log cabin school   _____ a small stone schoolhouse

_____ a school for wealthy children

Thinking Further

1. Do you like horses? Would you want to see a race? Why or why not?

2. Give Kentucky a nickname.

97

Answer Key

Answer Key

Reading Skills

1. Nevada is the _____ state in the United States.
   - _____ rainiest
   - __X__ driest
   - _____ hottest

2. Huge piles of cement were used to make Hoover Dam
   - __X__ strong. _____ gray. _____ cold.

3. Who was Hoover Dam named after?
   - _____ the person who built it
   - __X__ a president
   - _____ the governor of Nevada

4. The water in Lake Tahoe is
   - __X__ clear. _____ cloudy. _____ shallow.

Thinking Further

1. Would you want to live in Nevada? Why or why not?
2. Would you want to help build a giant water dam? Why or why not?

107

Reading Skills

1. Texas is so big that it has _____ time zones.
   - _____ three
   - __X__ two
   - _____ one

2. If you visit Big Bend National Park, what might you see?
   - __X__ bats
   - _____ bears
   - _____ baboons

3. Why did the author write this article?
   - _____ to tell about armadillos
   - __X__ to tell about the state of Texas
   - _____ to make the reader laugh

Thinking Further

1. Would you want to live in Texas? Why or why not?
2. If you visited, what animal would you most like to see?

109

Reading Skills

1. Over _____ islands make up Hawaii.
   - __X__ one hundred
   - _____ two hundred
   - _____ three hundred

2. The word aloha means
   - _____ like. _____ pretty. __X__ love.

3. Volcanoes make Hawaii's
   - __X__ islands. _____ weather. _____ oceans.

4. Saying aloha is a way to _____ people.
   - _____ confuse
   - __X__ welcome
   - _____ call

Thinking Further

1. Would you want to live in Hawaii? Why or why not?
2. Would you want to tour a volcano?
3. What is unusual about some of the plants and animals in Hawaii?
   They are not found anywhere else.

111

Reading Skills

1. What might you see in Maryland?
   - __X__ bays
   - _____ a rain forest
   - _____ the tallest mountain

2. Maryland has things to do for
   - __X__ everybody. _____ a few people.

3. Which of these is Maryland's nickname?
   - _____ "little America" _____ "the Bay State"
   - __X__ "mini America"

4. Francis Scott Key was on a _____ in a harbor when he wrote America's anthem.
   - _____ plane __X__ boat _____ beach

Thinking Further

1. Would you like to live in Maryland? Why or why not?
2. What would you nickname Maryland?
3. How do you think Maryland got its nickname?
   Possible answer: It has mountains, valleys, and beaches, just like America does.

113

Answer Key

Reading Skills

1. What might you see in California?

   X movie making   _____ cornfields

   _____ kangaroos

2. Why do so many people visit California?

   X There are many pretty places to visit.

   _____ There are lots of cars.

   _____ There are lots of people.

3. Based on the article, you know that California is near

   X the ocean.   _____ Florida.   _____ a big lake.

4. **California is the largest state.** Is this true or false?

   _____ true   X false

Thinking Further

1. Would you like to live in California? Why or why not?

2. What would you nickname California?

3. Look at the picture near the top of this page. What does it help you understand about California?

   How big redwood trees are.

115

Reading Skills

1. What might you see in Florida?

   _____ polar bears

   X alligators

   _____ bears

2. What fruit is grown a lot in Florida?

   _____ bananas   _____ apples   X oranges

3. In paragraph 2, what does the word *launched* mean?

   _____ moved   X sent into the air   _____ stored

4. Based on the pictures, what kinds of trees do you think grow in Florida?

   X palm trees   _____ redwood trees   _____ birch trees

Thinking Further

1. Would you like to live in Florida? Why or why not?

2. What nickname would you give Florida?

3. Tell what you know or have heard about hurricanes.

117

Reading Skills

1. What might you see in New York?

   X the Statue of Liberty   _____ the Painting of Liberty

   _____ the Statue of Freedom

2. Why might it be fun to visit New York City?

   X There are a lot of fun things to do.

   _____ It is sunny.

   _____ There are a lot of roads.

3. Which of these best describes New York?

   _____ a small city   X a busy city   _____ a country town

4. New York has more _____ than any other American city.

   _____ statues   X people   _____ buses

Thinking Further

1. Would you like to visit New York? Why or why not?

2. What would you nickname New York?

3. When people are new to America, why do you think they go to New York?

119

Reading Skills

1. What might you see in Pennsylvania?

   X the Liberty Bell

   _____ the Statue of Liberty

   _____ the Liberty Well

2. Philadelphia is a city where famous people signed

   _____ baseball cards.   X important papers.   _____ art.

3. Who is Pennsylvania named after?

   X William Penn

   _____ Sylvia Penn

   _____ Ben Franklin

4. Which of these is NOT a city in Pennsylvania?

   _____ Pittsburgh   _____ Philadelphia   X Penn City

Thinking Further

1. Would you learn a lot by going to Philadelphia? Why or why not?

2. What are two words to describe Pennsylvania?

3. Tell what you know about the Declaration of Independence.

121

Answer Key

Reading Skills

1. Mount Rushmore has _____ faces carved out of stone.

_____ three

_____ two

__X__ four

2. The Badlands are

_____ bad.   _____ good.   __X__ filled with gorges.

3. Whose faces are carved in Mount Rushmore?

_____ hikers   __X__ presidents   _____ athletes

4. What is a mesa?

_____ a desert

_____ a lake

__X__ a hill with a flat top

Thinking Further

1. Would you want to see Mount Rushmore? Why or why not?

2. Do you think it would be hard to carve people's heads out of stone? Why or why not?

123

Reading Skills

1. What president was born in Virginia?

__X__ George Washington

_____ George Bush

_____ King George

2. What was the name of the first English town?

__X__ Jamestown

_____ Jimstown

3. The first English __town__ was built in Virginia.
park town barn

Thinking Further

1. Would you like to visit Virginia? Why or why not?

2. What do you think you might see in an old fashioned town like Williamsburg?

3. In the second paragraph, it says that Jamestown was founded in 1607. What do you think *founded* means?

Possible answer: started; begun

125

Reading Skills

1. Winters in Minnesota can be so cold that wet hair turns to

_____ snow.

__X__ ice.

_____ dark.

2. Where might you go swimming in Minnesota?

__X__ lakes   _____ parks   _____ oceans

3. The cities of Minneapolis and St. Paul are known as the

_____ "Double Cities."   __X__ "Twin Cities."

_____ "Chilly Cities."

4. Fishing and boating are fun to do in Minnesota during the

_____ winter.   __X__ summer.

Thinking Further

1. Would you want to visit Minnesota? Why or why not?

2. What are two words that describe Minnesota?

3. If you lived in Minnesota, would you like summer or winter better? Why?

127

Reading Skills

1. The city of Denver is _____ in the sky.

_____ low

__X__ high

_____ blue

2. Some people come to this state to

__X__ ski.   _____ surf.   _____ see fish.

3. What is the capital of Colorado?

_____ Rocky Mountain

_____ Mile City

__X__ Denver

Thinking Further

1. Would you like to ski, bike, or raft in Colorado? Why?

2. What are two words to describe Colorado?

3. What does the red star by Denver on the map mean?

It means that Denver is the capital of Colorado.

129

Spectrum Reading Grade 1

154

Answer Key

Answer Key

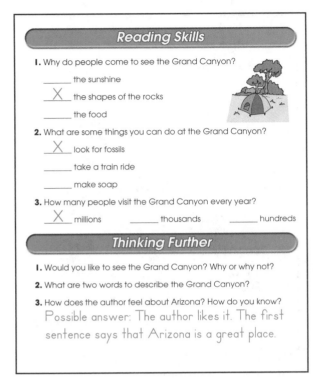

Reading Skills

1. Why do people come to see the Grand Canyon?
   _____ the sunshine
   __X__ the shapes of the rocks
   _____ the food

2. What are some things you can do at the Grand Canyon?
   __X__ look for fossils
   _____ take a train ride
   _____ make soap

3. How many people visit the Grand Canyon every year?
   __X__ millions _____ thousands _____ hundreds

Thinking Further

1. Would you like to see the Grand Canyon? Why or why not?

2. What are two words to describe the Grand Canyon?

3. How does the author feel about Arizona? How do you know?
   Possible answer: The author likes it. The first sentence says that Arizona is a great place.

131

Words to Know

1. (duck) dog did
2. for (fish) from
3. (grass) green go
4. (bowl) bee big
5. call can't (cold)
6. (water) wet won't
7. (pond) put play
8. (foot) farm for
9. can class (corn)
10. hop (hat) him
11. (road) run red
12. (sun) son sit
13. pull push (pail)
14. (soft) set says
15. sleep slip (sled)

132

Words to Know

1. snap (snail) snore
2. has (hand) her
3. pine (penny) pinch
4. was (wing) wish
5. (fox) for from
6. (dinner) dime don't
7. am apple (ape)
8. want (wish) will
9. (whale) wink what
10. friend (feet) from
11. (fly) fry fun
12. (sun) star skip
13. kit (kite) kiss
14. (gift) give get
15. (string) step skunk

133

Contractions

can't   didn't
won't   let's
don't   that's
isn't   I'll
wasn't

1. do not _don't_
2. let us _let's_
3. will not _won't_
4. was not _wasn't_
5. is not _isn't_
6. that is _that's_
7. can not _can't_
8. did not _didn't_
9. I will _I'll_

134

Answer Key

Lost Letters

1. Why does Little Duck want to fly?

   He wants to see the blue s_k_y.

2. How can he fly?

   With his w_i_ngs.

3. Do boys and girls have wings?

   N_o_t that I can se_e_.

4. Do fish have wings?

   N_o_, but they have f_i_ns.

5. Can Little Duck dive?

   Yes, he can d_i_ve.

135

Lost Letters

1. What animal did Carolyn pick?

   She picked a k_i_tten.

2. How did the kitten feel?

   The new kitten felt s_o_ft.

3. What kind of pets do most people have?

   Most people have c_a_ts or d_o_gs.

4. Do some people have different pets?

   Max has a pet fr_o_g and a pet t_u_rtle.

5. Would a tiger make a good pet?

   No, a tiger wo_n_'t make a good pet.

136

Words to Know

1. hall / (home) / hop
2. (bear) / bee / big
3. pat / (pet) / pit
4. (green) / great / good
5. bench / (boat) / belt
6. like / (love) / log
7. to / (two) / toe
8. bend / (back) / bath
9. big / bring / (bow)
10. bars / (bug) / birds
11. (call) / can't / can
12. (land) / lick / lip
13. can / (cage) / call
14. (play) / pan / pin
15. ran / run / (rock)

137

Notes